The Knucklebook

*Everything You Need to Know About
Baseball's Strangest Pitch—the Knuckleball*

Dave Clark

Drawings by Patrick Clark

Ivan R. Dee
Chicago

THE KNUCKLEBOOK. Copyright © 2006 by Dave Clark. All rights reserved, including the right to reproduce this book or portions thereof in any form. For information, address: Ivan R. Dee, Publisher, 1332 North Halsted Street, Chicago 60622. Manufactured in the United States of America and printed on acid-free paper.

www.ivanrdee.com

Library of Congress Cataloging-in-Publication Data:
Clark, Dave, 1952–
  The knucklebook : everything you need to know about baseball's
  strangest pitch—the knuckleball / Dave Clark ; drawings by
  Patrick Clark
    p. cm.
  Includes index.
  ISBN 1-56663-661-2 (cloth : alk. paper)
  1. Pitching (Baseball) I. Clark, Patrick. II. Title.
GV871.C53 2006
796.357'22—dc

                                        2005021245

This book is dedicated to the guy who showed me my very first knuckleball. I'll never get over it, Dad.

Preface

This book will teach you all you need to know about the most frustrating yet entertaining pitch in baseball: the knuckleball.

It frustrates batters when it works; it embarrasses pitchers when it doesn't . . . or if it works all too well. It humiliates catchers and umpires. It confounds spectators.

This book will explain the strange workings and use of the knuckleball, no matter what your interest. It offers enough information to satisfy you, no matter what your viewpoint may be. For umpires this book offers little— but enough to enable them to do their best under mind-numbing circumstances. For catchers and batters it reveals a little more useful detail, maybe enough to save a career. For pitchers it offers a lot, with obvious possibilities of world-class mastery even at the mid-teen level. For spectators . . . just hope that knuckleball pitcher on your team has taken this information to heart.

This information has been gathered from many sources—professional and amateur, casual observers and physics wizards. I found it easy to interview Hoyt Wilhelm, even though the legendary sportswriter Joe Falls says Wilhelm was his toughest interview. All I did was ask him questions until I found some he wanted to answer. I got more than one nugget from him, which was plenty for me. Knuckleball pitchers individually have few details, but collectively they offer a rich treasury of fun and useful information.

This book is written so that most anyone can understand it and benefit, and worded so that a reader who might use it will understand the point, even if a pure technician may disagree with my explanation. Not everyone can put this information to use, however; like throwing a dart at a bull's-eye, it takes intelligent practice—ten minutes to teach, but a lifetime to learn. It's said that only about 2 percent of fastball pitchers "get it"; this applies to knuckleball pitchers as well.

Misinformation is disproved here as well as opinion that doesn't hold up to the evidence. So many people are throwing so many floaters in so many ways that just scouring the knuckleball's long history tells us that new techniques and grips are yet to reveal themselves. There is more to the knuckleball than even I realized when I started this project. What I have here now, though, ought to be helpful to anyone. So enjoy it.

Oh, and with apologies to Bill O'Reilly, *this* is the real No-Spin Zone.

Acknowledgments

You could probably guess most of those I should give credit to. I'll name all I can anyway.

Dad showed me my first one, bless his soul in heaven. If you can make a baseball do that wacky stuff, you earn your place on high.

With sufficient time I could likely assemble a knuckle-baller family tree, to show who begat who in the pantheon of major league pitching. I'd prefer to voice my thanks to those who provided a gem or two, whether I spoke to them personally or heard secondhand how they tossed one out for all flutterball fans to admire.

And so I thank Phil Niekro, who gave this temporarily transplanted Red Sox fan a reason to cheer for a player of a different uniform. Phil, you're still showing a lot of us how to do it, and Cooperstown is honored.

Hoyt Wilhelm was kindly regarded as "irascible." I thought better of him, probably because I understood what he must have been made of, to throw this nonsense high school-velocity balloon and make a living at it, baffling professional hitters all the way to the Hall of Fame. Many wear his number 49 in his honor, and for obvious reason. He told me, "You gotta be smart to throw it." No brag there, just a vital fact.

Charlie Hough may be the best one I haven't gotten to speak with, and he may be able to coach it better than most former major league butterfly artists. I've heard from others more than a few of his prime cuts, and relating this pitch to regular baseball seems to be natural for him. I like your commonsense point of view, Charlie.

Tom Candiotti phoned me. This was part of a service where celebrities are paid to drop you a line with a brief canned greeting, but things got past that fast. Tom, do call me again, on my dime. You're sharper at color commentary than others give you credit for, and I'll take whatever abuse you may give me for what you don't agree with here.

Tim Wakefield, more than anyone else, is now showing more amused wannabes how to baffle the best batters. The fact that he often is the *only* major leaguer throwing the knuckleball has something to do with that, but he does have to confound them often enough to keep his job. When he's on, it's astonishing to watch this man have such an easy day at the office. When he's off, however, he's demonstrating the potential whimsy of the ball as it approaches enemy batters who see lunch coming. Tim, you can call me too; I have another dime just for you. Even though you're headed for the rocking chair, as ballplayers do at your age, you'll at least find it fun to chat—I guarantee.

Nothing is more fun than talking to the game's best lefty knuckleballer, Wilbur Wood. Mr. Wood, you're all class. You still don't get the credit you deserve. You were a horse when throwing loads of innings was nothing to notice; today you'd stun the baseball world, so your only knock is arriving on the planet thirty years too soon. You'd get the Cy Young just for showing up for work as often as you used to.

Matthew Crowder gave me webspace and helped this rookie webmaster along, and he came up with the idea of a message board. This was probably the knuckleball's biggest breakthrough in my lifetime, because it allowed the scattered few endangered cuckoos to connect . . . and they have. Somehow the worldwide web is the communication version of a Barry White album, because the knuckleball seems to be arising anew, in all manner of scattered locales. If you watch for the important and eye-popping details, you'll see that some of these young scruffs have the magic act down to match major league legends. Zach Staniewicz dared to toss a knuckler as a ceremonial first pitch at a Lowell (Massachusetts) Spinners A-ball game. I have to believe he'll wind up throwing more someday, for real, for a paycheck, if given the chance. Sean Flaherty didn't get drafted, as two major national magazines suggested. As a consolation prize, he has a ticket for an extended stretch at the University of Miami. Consolation? As a high schooler he was coaching a minor league pitcher or two on the finer points. Already he's had the highest highs and lowest lows that are the mark of a wizened old hand at the knuckleball. It's good that he got those out of the way in his teens and not in mid-career, in his twenties and thirties, like most.

My son, Patrick, figured it out and threw it in high school, despite my coaching. The best two teachers are also the best two students, provided they're attempting to play catch with it in the driveway. So I guess he taught me as much as I taught him. Watching him made me regret I wasn't in his position at his age. I'm still proud to have seen all those goofy things fly out of his hands over the years. Part of what I explain here is what I observed myself, just trying to pitch it as well as he does.

Bill George e-mailed me out of the blue, suggesting I write this book. Actually his first idea was a DVD, which may come later. He taught me fast that when you do things by yourself, you're alone. In other words, anyone deciding to self-produce a product may have a fool for a marketing staff. Bill, be glad all I bounced off you were ideas. They may not bruise as much as quarter-pound baseballs.

There are the usual too many others to thank, not only at my website, www.knuckleballhq.com, but in my personal life. Friends and family have supported me in this project, generally by ignoring me as I go off to a corner to do Dave things, this being the silliest to them. We'll see.

This book will unearth new butterfly pitchers and maybe find enough of a following so I can leave my day job and help develop those who could use an idea or three. My wife, Ann, and daughter, Kayley, my mom and other friends and relatives would appreciate that. So would all those pros-in-training, and so would I. I'll be forever astonished and grateful that the publisher, Ivan R. Dee, went looking for me, and personally and professionally walked me through this adventure in prose.

Finally, I have to acknowledge the sports fans everywhere who came out of the woodwork and—cracking a little smile—voiced their interest in what's here. This book is not about the author; it's about them. I just wasted a lot of time over the years, maniacally added to my collection of knuckleball information, then discovered to my amazement how many wanted me to report back with all the magician's black-art secrets. Lest you think I'm spoiling the trick, just remember one thing: can you throw it for strikes?

If not, well, understand that the knuckleball amuses everyone in some fashion. So I present this book to you, the legion of fans of this comedy baseball pitch. It's a joke you can share with everyone, and the punch line never gets as old as those who eventually master it.

D. C.

Barre, Massachusetts
October 2005

Contents

The Knucklebook

· 1 ·

How a Knuckleball Knuckles

To understand how to pitch to win, you have to understand physics, aerodynamics, and ball rotation. Knowing how to use them to your advantage helps you counter the forces of nature. Like every human who ever lived, you have to respect, plan for, and deal with the pull of gravity, the laws of momentum, and the atmosphere we live in. No matter how great a pitcher you are, you can't overcome the laws of physical nature—but you can toy with them, to the frustration of anyone holding a baseball bat.

Most of what you can do with a baseball involves those marvelous little stitches—their shape, size, orientation, and rotation. If those stitches did not exist, the game would be very different. Most pitchers use the skilled spin of those stitches to do their job; a knuckleballer uses little or no spin to do his. This book explains the magic world that baseball becomes when those stitches don't spin normally.

Have you ever been in a small boat and noticed the little knots of water that swirl in the boat's wake? Air going around a baseball produces this very same effect, seen best in a wind tunnel. (You can find much more information about coefficients of drag, fluid dynamics, and Reynolds numbers. To understand the action of the knuckleball in technical terms, check out the work of some of these noted experts: Dr. Joel Hollenberg, Robert K. Adair, Robert G. Watts and Eric Sawyer, Kai Tang, Adam Kleinbaum, and Dane Shellhouse.) As an object moves through the air, air is compressed along all sides of it, especially in front. This produces drag on the object where the air is compressed.

Air doesn't slide along solid surfaces very well, but air easily slides over pockets of air moving in other directions. This is the key to producing the knuckleball effect on a baseball. The seams on a baseball act like the air dam underneath the front of a car. The air dam pushes the air aside and forms swirls (a vortex) of air that move in all kinds of directions around all the car parts behind the air dam. These swirls act like ball bearings, allowing the nearby air stream to flow smoothly past. Without the air dam, the air would drag across all those parts.

The stitches on a baseball push the air flow away from the ball's leather surface just enough to form tiny swirls of air behind them.

Air moving faster across a surface produces lower pressure than air moving more slowly elsewhere on the same surface. An airplane wing works that way: air pushed aside by the curve on top has to move fast to meet up with the air moving along the straight bottom, so pressure is lower on top and the wing has lift. Low pressure draws the object toward it, so wherever the lowest pressure is on that object from moment to moment, that's where the object will drift to. This is related to the Magnus effect. It does not have much effect on a baseball, but air currents sliding behind the ball—faster and easier in some places than others—can have a strong effect on the wake behind it.

What greatly affects the movement of a baseball is the size, shape, and location of that wake behind it, which causes enough drag to change the path of the ball. When a pitcher throws a fastball, the pitch spins rapidly, allowing this wake to fill and keeping it relatively small. You might think of this effect as using the seams to pump a flow of air toward a particular area behind the ball. There the airflow may develop some lift—as on a four-seam fastball, or slightly less on a two-seamer (which doesn't present as many seams to keep the wake as small), or some drag to one side as with a curve ball. This effect is easily apparent on a rapidly rotating ball, as shown here:

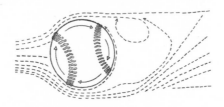

This ball is moving through the air from right to left, and is rotating rapidly across the top, in the direction of the plate. It appears that this is pumping air across the top, helping to fill in the wake in a predictable and steady manner. The actual airflow around a spinning ball may not look exactly like this, but it will always keep the same look throughout its path from pitcher to target, and similar rotation with each pitch will produce the same effect.

In the action of the knuckleball, however, some stitches are moving toward the flow of air in front, and others are moving away, *at a slow speed*. The stitches move around the ball in quite a complex curve on a knuckleball, and the ball may rotate at different rates in different ways. This causes the swirls of air to change size and direction, form and disappear, and move location on the ball, thus producing changing locations of low pressure that really can't be predicted. The wake behind a single knuckleball, moving from right to left, at various points in flight may look like this:

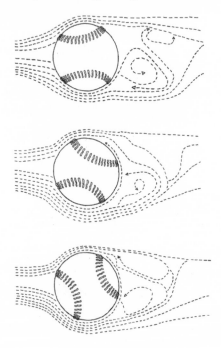

Fast rotation can partially counteract gravity. A hard-thrown fastball rotating front to back, as shown on page 19, produces lift just behind and slightly above the center of the ball, tending to hold it up so that gravity doesn't drop it so quickly. A ball with little if any rotation doesn't generate that lift, and it produces a larger wake, maybe a foot or longer, so it naturally falls away. This explains the drop of a knuckleball (and, similarly, the forkball or split-finger fastball). Also, the sudden growth of the wake acts like a brake, suddenly slowing the ball. If it happens to be moving to one side at the time, the ball may suddenly dive off to that side. It's the rapid change of the shape and size of the wake behind the knuckleball that produces the odd movement.

Picture this: imagine a Chihuahua with its tail; that's a fastball. Now, imagine a Chihuahua with a German shepherd's tail; that's a knuckleball. A slowly rotating ball can develop a very large tail, which can wag the dog! That's a knuckleball . . . it gets wagged by its tail. Here are overhead views of the possible flight paths of two knuckleballs.

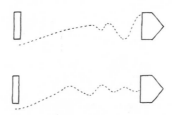

Phil Niekro is a Hall of Fame pitcher and one of the best knucklers ever. Measurements of Niekro's pitch concluded that a knuckleball moves the most at around 72 miles per hour. Knuckleballs at about that speed have been measured to move as much as 18 inches off line! Home plate is only 17 inches wide.

Slower knuckleballs start moving at around 50 miles per hour and usually exhibit just some drop. Very fast knuckleballs almost vibrate before they drop at the last moment, because they don't move much side to side. Faster knuckleballs, since they arrive at the plate quicker, also have less time to move very much, and the fast air stream tends to keep them in line; slower ones, thrown in a tall curving arc, have more time to vibrate, shake, drop and dance side to side, and have less air pressure around them to keep them in a straight line.

Now, there's one influence no one talks about that explains why a nonrotating knuckleball may still swoop all over the place. I call this the Ferris wheel effect.

Ride a Ferris wheel and notice that although you always face forward, the air comes from above as you rise, then it shifts to the front as you reach the top, then from below as you ride down the front.

A knuckleball, thrown slowly in a big arc, "sees" the wind from slightly above the front-center, then directly in front, then slightly below front-center. This movement of the "relative wind" along the front of the ball will naturally produce shifts in where and how those stitch-produced swirls happen, and therefore the size and shape of the ball's wake. It's known that only a small rotation of a knuckleball, as little as 15 degrees, can produce a huge change in this wake. That's why practiced knuckleball

pitchers who can reduce the ball's spin experiment with
different orientations of the ball in their hand to produce
the ideal action for them personally—maybe with less than
predictable results. Some position their fingers to produce
a "horseshoe" facing front; others grip the ball where the
seams come closest together; and most monkey around
with multiple variations. This is easy to show: look at
these two baseballs. The difference is a turn of only 15
degrees.

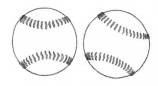

This is what the wind in front of the ball "sees," so you can
understand that one position creates its own movement,
and a different position as slight as this produces something entirely different.

There is no ideal rotation distance or speed. The numbers indicate that it takes only a few degrees of rotation
difference from ball to ball to produce entirely different
action. Knuckleball pitchers have generally arrived at
less than a half-turn of the ball on its way to the plate as
necessary to get it to do strange things. Add that to differences in pitch speeds, wind direction and speed,
humidity, and altitude, and you have a totally unpredictable pitch as well as the near impossibility of producing the same action from pitch to pitch.

A good way to judge what may be good enough low rotation is this: when you throw a knuckleball, can you see the

stitches? If you can, you've probably cut the rotation down enough to produce a good knuckler. It has been demonstrated, though, that if the ball rotates slightly clockwise or counterclockwise, and the stitches are aligned properly from the start, this may produce a spiral shape to the wake behind the ball, producing a ball that actually corkscrews! Hoyt Wilhelm called it his "spinner," it's believed. Also, throwing into a strong wind produces more air speed. The ball may move a *lot* more, compressing its action into a much shorter distance. A real catcher's nightmare! This is why many a knuckleball pitcher likes a little breeze in his face. Seeing the stitches and maybe even the writing on a ball can produce a hypnotic effect on a batter, but to see the ball make several unexpected darts and bumps with a dive at the end, well, sometimes that Louisville Slugger won't be of much use.

Often a knuckleball moves or jumps only a few inches, but that's enough to mess up a batter. Spectators, many feet away and often off to one side, have an impossible time judging any side-to-side movement from that distance and angle. But what counts most is that the batter will have a hard time getting the sweet spot of the bat on this ball. The pitch isn't ending up where he thinks it will, so he has to make unusual adjustments in his swing just to make contact. Even a tiny variation in a smooth swing is enough to cause the hitter to miss the pitch or not make solid contact. This will result in a weak grounder or pop-up.

Atmospheric conditions do have an effect on the knuckleball, but not as most people think. Denser air, such as you'd get on hot and humid days, will allow the ball to move more. Altitude generally does not affect it as much as air density. Pros like Tim Wakefield like to throw in domes because the air is controlled; to keep them from turning into saunas from the lights and body heat of all those fans, the HVAC systems keep the air circulating in a predictable manner. If the air is predictable, a good knuckleball pitcher can usually adjust to it quickly. Throwing into a hard breeze, besides essentially compressing the movement of the ball, forces the pitcher to pay more attention to guiding the pitch home, as opposed to throwing it. I once threw one into the teeth of a howling wind, right past my nephew, who just stood there and stared in wide-eyed amazement as it *corkscrewed* past him. I accidentally snapped my wrist off to the outside at exactly the right moment at release, which put a light outside rotation on the ball. Other pitchers have thrown these corkscrews, and as soon as we figure out how to throw them consistently, we'll have one killer *easily locatable* knuckleball, predictable to the pitcher but not to the batter. Some pitchers, like Red Sox prospect Charlie Zink, report they can get the ball to sink off to one side or another with a bit of predictability by orienting the stitches particular ways. But until we get so skilled we can throw any kind we want, we'll all have to pitch like Phil Niekro did: just throw it at the catcher's mask and cheer for it on the way in.

As there's a psychological advantage to throwing a hypnotic and mind-numbing pitch, so too is there an advantage to using a grip and seam orientation that you're comfortable with. Confidence in what you're throwing takes you a long way. Poise on the mound can be obvious, and that can have an additional intimidating effect on opposing batters. And it can make throwing a so-called tough pitch much easier.

· 2 ·

The Knuckleball versus Everything Else

"Like some cult religion that barely survives, there has always been at least one but rarely more than five or six devotees throwing the knuckleball in the big leagues. Not only can't pitchers control it, hitters can't hit it, catchers can't catch it, coaches can't coach it, and most pitchers can't learn it. The perfect pitch."—Ron Luciano, former American League umpire.

The most basic decision a batter has to make when a pitch comes his way is to decide if it's a ball or strike. If he thinks it's a strike, he then has to decide if he can put the sweet spot of the bat on the ball and drive it. Therefore it usually makes sense to throw a pitch to a particular spot to try to fool that batter.

All that goes out the window if the pitch is a knuckleball.

The four most important elements of a pitch are, in order of importance: location, change of pace, movement, and velocity. We'll discuss them in detail later. The three main cornerstones of any pitching game plan are to throw strikes, mix speeds, and usually keep the ball down. What's important here is how a knuckleball enters into these tactics and messes up the batter's normal split-second decision-making.

The batter is looking for a pitch in a particular location because he's learned to hit balls well when they are in particular places in the strike zone. Some batters are good low-ball hitters; some are good high-ball hitters. Most hit well when they get a ball down the middle. They do some adjusting if they decide to swing at a ball that's not going quite where they thought, and if they're quick enough, they check their swing, especially if the ball is headed outside the strike zone. They also make an adjustment if the ball arrives sooner or later than they expect. Most batters, therefore, are going to the plate looking for a pitch in a particular location and at a particular speed. This may change depending on the ball/strike count, or the number of outs, or the number of players on base, or the score, or the inning.

One clue a batter has is to watch how the ball is spinning. Since different pitches rotate in different ways, that spin may signal a fastball, curve, slider, or other pitch. It may confirm that the pitch coming is what he's waiting for, and all he has to do is judge whether it will end up where he likes it.

But what does a batter do when a pitch suddenly is not only much slower than he expects, but is also moving side-to-side in strange ways, and maybe sinking like a rock at the last moment? And he sees the stitches on the ball so well he can almost count them? Maybe he can't do much!

Here's an eye-opening fact: *Most average middle school pitchers have the same velocity as an established veteran major league knuckleball pitcher.* So what's the difference? Learning to make adjustments as conditions change, so you're not just a successful knuckleball pitcher, you're a successful pitcher who happens to throw knuckleballs. It's possible for a talented middle school pitcher to pitch *exactly* like an established major league knuckleballer, years before he makes the majors.

Obviously a pitcher can't throw a knuckleball to a spot in the strike zone, and he can't depend on the standard speed he may expect from another kind of pitch. But this is also a problem for any batter who has gotten used to other pitches. Like other pitches, the pitcher knows what's about to be delivered, and the batter does not. And because a knuckleball is so unpredictable, it can be thrown many times in a row—unlike most other pitches.

One advantage to a knuckleball is how it is thrown in relation to faster pitches. A knuckleball—or any other off-speed pitch—is highly effective at the Little League level, simply because even a bad one thrown slower than the fastballs the batter sees is hard to adjust to at that age. A Little League pitcher can do well by throwing a lot of fastballs for strikes and mixing in a so-so knuckleball when a change-up pitch will work. At this level a pitcher doesn't have to throw a knuckleball that swoops all over the place. In fact, one that does that may be the *wrong* pitch to throw, because it is especially difficult for catchers at that skill level to catch a pitch outside the strike zone, never mind one that shifts one way and another.

So if a Little Leaguer can throw fastball strikes consistently and would like to add an off-speed pitch for extra effectiveness, it's perfectly okay to try a few knuckleballs now and then, especially if they're thrown noticeably slower, and still thrown for strikes.

Every pitcher who is thinking about throwing a knuckleball in a game should heed the advice of Tom Candiotti: a knuckleball will never make up for bad pitching. You can never be a better pitcher by throwing a knuckleball unless you're already a good pitcher. I once coached a Babe Ruth player who came off his first-ever few innings on the mound quite exhilarated at what he had done, even though it was a so-so performance at best. He basically had only a four-seam fastball, and he didn't throw a great percentage for strikes. He wanted me to teach him a curveball, and I had to turn him down. It's no different when considering a knuckleball.

Sure, because you don't fire them as hard as you would fastballs, you can throw more knuckleballs for a long time. For a knuckleballer, a pitch count of 150 is not a problem. Unless it's the first inning. Bad knuckleball pitchers get shelled fast. Average ones get nickel-and-dimed to death with off-field bloops, walks, passed balls, and infield dribblers. Great ones have a solid strikeout-to-walk ratio (2 to 1 or better), keep the walks and passed balls way down, and know exactly what to do to get strikes and make it a good day at the office. This explains in part why knuckleball pitchers often arrive in the major leagues at a more advanced age than most. They've generally had to figure all this out themselves, because there has been so little coaching and understanding of how to apply this unusual pitch to game play at the major league level, as well as difficulty in learning how to keep it around the strike zone. The best knuckleball pitchers usually got better once they could hobnob with a fellow wizard, who had also discovered tricks of his own. Outside of that, no one knew much about it.

Pitchers at any level who have a knuckleball should continue to work mainly on fastball mechanics. When they are older and more skilled, solid fastball mechanics will be greatly helpful if they want to continue to throw knuckleballs. (The use of fastball mechanics in throwing a knuckleball is explained later.)

If you never throw a knuckleball, or if you throw almost all knuckleballs, you must still stick to the three cornerstones of the pitching plan: Throw strikes. Mix speeds. Usually keep the ball down.

Remember the four main elements of any one pitch: location, change of pace, movement, and velocity? They don't seem to mean much if you are throwing a lot of knuckleballs, but at an advanced level they do.

An accomplished knuckleball pitcher can locate the pitch up or down at various heights in the strike zone, but that's pretty much it for location. If the knuckleballs are noticeably slower than what the batter is used to, the change of pace is effective until the time comes when a different speed pitch is called for. Movement—well, you'll get plenty of that on a knuckleball, but it might be too much for the catcher to handle. Velocity is an advantage when the pitch is so fast that the batter can't adjust; it's not an advantage when the batter can meet the ball squarely and drive it a mile with ease. Lack of velocity is an advantage too—when the batter can't adjust to pitches much slower than normal—and that should be easy to use. Those who know pitching in-depth know that high velocity is overrated and change of velocity is underrated; understanding this, and knowing how to use this understanding to pitch effectively, is the ultimate goal of every knuckleball pitcher.

Some pitchers use a knuckleball as an off-speed pitch when they quickly get ahead of the batter, such as with an 0-2 count. Bobby Shantz, a shorter-than-average pitcher, had a monster year pitching that very way. Nothing wrong with that! Another way even a lame knuckleball can be highly useful: the first-pitch strike. Any pitcher does himself a huge favor by throwing first-pitch strikes as often as possible. Batters usually take the first one, but for pitchers there's the additional rule that the first pitch shouldn't be too good—just in case the batter is ready and willing to go after it. Even a bad knuckleball thrown as a first-pitch strike can confuse a batter the rest of the at-bat, especially if he has no idea how to adjust to hit one. Whatever you throw for a first pitch, try to make it a strike, and one that isn't too tempting to hit.

Oddly enough, because a knuckleball is so unpredictable, location has a lot to do with throwing it effectively. You can't locate a knuckleball with pinpoint accuracy, but because it does what it does, it's an effective location pitch. If a pitch moves just a few inches up or down the length of the bat away from the sweet spot, and does that too unpredictably for the batter to adjust, you have an effective pitch. Or if it drops just a couple of inches or more at the last moment, the batter may miss the ball entirely. A knuckleball may do both, and at the same time, and over and over again.

Is there such a thing as a "pure" knuckleball pitcher? No. Everyone who has ever thrown it has had at least one other pitch. You had better be able to throw at least a fastball, because you need at least one pitch you can put where you need it. By itself that fastball may be lame, but mixed with knuckleballs it looks different. Some knuckleball pitchers have curves or sliders, or more. It was said that Phil Niekro's pitches, other than his knuckleballs, were pretty average. But he really knew how to mix them up to play with a batter's head. In his three hundredth win, he threw knuckleballs only at the very end of his nine-inning shutout. The opposing team kept looking for knuckleballs that never showed up! *That* is pitching! It's generally regarded that a "pure" knuckleball pitcher throws them as his bread-and-butter pitch more than 80 percent of the time.

How does a knuckle-curve enter into this? It doesn't. It's a true curveball, thrown much like a two-seam fastball except that the index finger is curled under so the middle finger gets the entire grip along a seam off to one side of center. Burt Hooton allegedly ended up with one while he was young and trying to develop his own knuckleball from sketchy information. His was a knuckleball grip held low, his fingers flicking the top of the ball, so it had a light forward roll off to one side. It sank hard and curved, so some called it a knuckle-curve. It was actually a locatable form of knuckleball because it had a different grip, delivery, and action from those of a knuckle-curve.

What about splitters and forkballs? They're close relatives of the knuckleball. They're thrown with fingers spread wide on either side of the ball, oriented like a two-seam fastball, and thrown hard enough so that the batter won't have time to notice there's hardly any spin on the ball. Because it's supposed to have little spin, it will naturally sink, but because it's thrown hard like a fastball, air

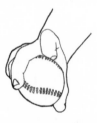

Knuckle-curve Grip

Forkball or Split-finger Fastball Grip

pressure on either side prevents it from moving much from side to side. This may have been the pitch that Toad Ramsey threw—it had knuckleball action without the knuckles. He may also have thrown one simply by gripping it low enough to allow it to slide upward out of his hand with some forward spin, like a spitter. Any knuckleball pitcher can try this.

Tim Wakefield says about the knuckleball, "When it's working, it's a lot of fun. I can imagine the batters saying to themselves, 'I can't hit that thing.'"

· 3 ·

How to Throw It

Few people learn the pitch from someone who has enough teaching expertise to pass along solid and dependable information. Learning the basics has generally come from hearing bits and pieces by hearsay or by reading a brief how-to somewhere, then many hours of backyard experimentation.

Surely some kids tried their hand at developing a knuckleball of their own when they found instructions in their pack of Goudey gum back in 1939 (see next page).

Jim Bouton worked out his version of a knuckleball after seeing a story about Dutch Leonard on the back of a Wheaties box. Here's Tim Wakefield's reply to my questions: "How did you learn it? Did you just keep experimenting until you got it?"

"The only thing I can tell you about how I learned is exactly how you described it. I just fooled around with it as a kid and eventually got good at throwing it consistently. Like they always say, practice makes perfect. Keep throwing it and don't let it spin."

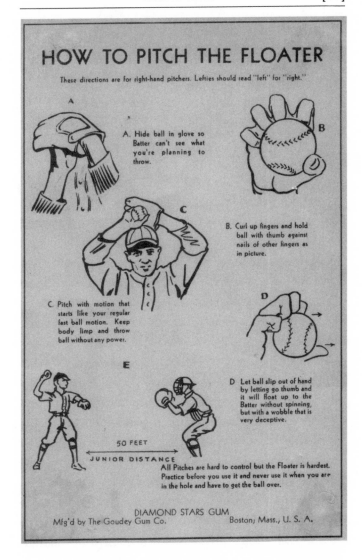

HOW TO PITCH THE FLOATER

These directions are for right-hand pitchers. Lefties should read "left" for "right."

A. Hide ball in glove so Batter can't see what you're planning to throw.

B. Curl up fingers and hold ball with thumb against nails of other fingers as in picture.

C. Pitch with motion that starts like your regular fast ball motion. Keep body limp and throw ball without any power.

D Let ball slip out of hand by letting go thumb and it will float up to the Batter without spinning, but with a wobble that is very deceptive.

50 FEET

JUNIOR DISTANCE

All Pitches are hard to control but the Floater is hardest. Practice before you use it and never use it when you are in the hole and have to get the ball over.

DIAMOND STARS GUM
Mfg'd by The Goudey Gum Co.   Boston, Mass., U. S. A.

I have gathered notes and advice from a wide number of pitchers; some are Hall of Famers, some had (and have) major league careers, and some are successful pros and amateurs in their own right. I have learned that some elements of throwing a knuckleball are almost universal from pitcher to pitcher, but unlike other pitches, there is always some individual style. I'll detail these here.

The Grip

The first time I met anyone skilled at throwing knuckleballs, he said one of the best things I've ever heard about the pitch. I asked Phil Niekro how he grips it, and he asked me in return, "Well, how do *you* grip it?" It really and truly is different for almost everyone in some ways, but there are almost universal elements. Most pitchers find the following elements to be part of their grip:

The ball is held snugly against the palm.

The thumb holds one side, and the end or side of another finger holds the ball *exactly* opposite the thumb.

One, two, or three fingers between the thumb and gripping finger are curled down onto the top of the ball and contact the ball with fingertips, fingernails, or knuckles.

It's thrown with a stiff wrist. *Do not* break the wrist until you're sure you've released the ball.

The ball is guided, *not pushed*, straight ahead, through the center, with the fingertips. If you do that correctly, the ball will leave your fingertips with little or no rotation, and you'll probably feel a slight "tick" off your curled fingernails.

That's it.

Phil Niekro describes the basic grip pretty much this way:

Place the ball on this spot.

Like so.

Grip with the thumb and side of the ring finger or little finger.

Lower two or three curled fingers to the top. Rest the fingertips comfortably on the ball.

Note the ball is gripped with the thumb and side of the ring finger (or little finger) and it stays tight against the palm.

Here's a bad grip. With the ball out in the fingers and away from the palm, you're probably going to get spin you don't like.

Here's the delivery:

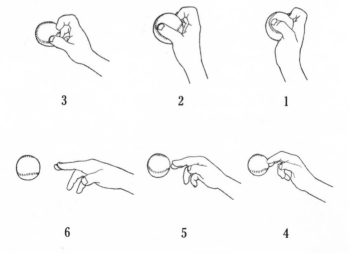

3   2   1

6   5   4

I've seen grips with fingernails dug into the ball or the seams. I've seen fingers curled over enough to get knuckles close to—or actually on—the ball. I've seen fingers curled only enough to touch the fingertip on the ball. I've seen grips with one, two, or three fingers curled a little or curled a lot, resting on top of the ball. Of all baseball pitches, the knuckleball grip is by far the most individual, because the pitcher has experimented before finding a grip that worked for *him*.

The grip is developed to accomplish one thing: to release the ball so it will move forward with little or no spin. Some pitchers can do this repeatedly by simply releasing fingers at the right time and in the right order. But many report that curled fingers allow them to release the ball with their thumb and opposite finger, and then feel the ball flick off their curled fingertips, as an indicator that they have stopped most of the ball's rotation.

Anyone who has found a successful grip quickly learns one thing: until release, they've generated velocity using essentially fastball mechanics. Therefore they can throw the ball pretty hard toward their target.

To prevent injury to the pitcher, one thing must be emphasized: a knuckleball is *thrown* to the target, not delivered like a shot put or pushed with the fingertips. The fingertip or fingernail "tick" that many knuckleballers report is there only to take any last-moment rotation off the ball. It tells the pitcher that those curled fingertips have come straight off the back of the ball as it is released, keeping rotation to a minimum. In other words, throw it with a solid and balanced windup and a stiff wrist, then release the thumb-and-finger-grip on the opposite side. When you feel the ball "tick" off the curled fingertips, you know you've probably thrown a good one. You can also imagine that you're trying to throw your curled fingertips through the back of the ball.

If you have large hands or long fingers or small hands, or you release ahead of yourself or next to your face, you'll have a different grip. Some people say they can't grip the ball well enough even to start to get their fingers curled down onto the ball, but by gripping with the thumb and side of the ring finger, you may find that even a small hand can get the middle fingertips down on the ball and grip it well enough to hold it against the palm.

Note that one almost universal part of the grip is holding the ball against the palm. You don't necessarily have to do this with a lot of pressure, but at least contacting the palm. Holding the ball even the slightest bit out in the fingers may prevent you from throwing it consistently—but this is not certain. Try it and find out for yourself. Holding it against the palm usually helps prevent the ball from even starting to rotate as it leaves your grip.

Some knuckleball pitchers say, "Don't grip the seams." Some say, "You need to trim your fingernails and keep them hard." Some say, "You need to push with your fingertips at the last moment." All these ideas work for *some* pitchers, but other pitchers have come up with strange grips that use the seams, or don't involve their fingernails much, or release and follow through much as they would a fastball. The only way you can find out what will work for you is by experimenting, sometimes long hours.

The only absolutes are that the ball should rotate very little (maybe a half-turn at most), and that it is *thrown*. *Many beginners are surprised to find just how fast 70 miles per hour is. That's the approximate velocity at which an experienced knuckleball pitcher can expect the most movement.*

Here are a few tips that may help you develop a knuckleball:

It's best not to watch the ball as you throw it. It's tempting, I know, but if you're throwing good ones, you'll know it two ways: you'll probably feel that finger tick, and your catcher will first laugh and then be panic-stricken. It really is best to have someone catching it and telling you what it's doing, for two simple reasons:

(1) You should be working on throwing strikes, no matter what you're throwing, so you should be looking at your target.

(2) All the action is happening increasingly farther away from you, and increasingly closer to your catcher. Almost always, your catcher will see more going on than you will. Where your catcher is setting up is where all the action that counts is happening.

Shifting a gripping finger just a quarter-inch away from a spot that worked for you may produce spin you can't stop. Some pitchers pick where they grip on the ball simply because the places where their fingers grip it are easy spots to remember and repeat. Advanced pitchers may find they get the movement and control they want by orienting the ball a particular way that has nothing to do with feeling for particular repeatable grip points. Over time you may change your grip when the one you have isn't quite doing the job.

Some coaches won't let their pitchers throw knuckle-balls because they claim it will hurt their arm. Well, throwing *anything* wrong will probably hurt. Too many kids and coaches don't get it and think it's thrown like a shot put, or pushed with the arm. That's way wrong.

Some coaches say it will slow the development of a pitcher's fastball. I can agree with that—almost. Learning solid fastball mechanics will teach you how to pitch with more power and less effort, prevent injuries, and develop endurance. It will teach you how to throw with control. You need those things first in order to throw knuckleballs.

Learning proper pitching while you are young and in a period of physical growth helps tremendously later on when you are grown. I know of one professional knuckle-ball pitcher who pretty much tops out with all his pitches in the mid-70s. Learning how to throw a harder, effective fastball at an early age would have allowed him to throw all his pitches faster, which would make his normal ones more confusing and effective. As in any physical activity, you should consult with a medical professional to prevent injury before you start.

The Basic Delivery

It's not much different from throwing a fastball, with two exceptions:

(1) Most knuckleballers plant their lead foot sooner and closer than they would with a fastball.

(2) Most finish standing straight up, facing straight ahead toward their target, with little follow-through with their pitching arm.

As with the fastball, you need to have a smooth, balanced, well-timed windup and rotation. But unlike a fastball delivery, you can't generate that extra power when the ball is coming forward with your pitching arm and your body propelling your pitching shoulder around and forward. Your pitching motion is simpler than that for a fastball, but because there is less to it, there is less opportunity for you to make up for an accidental hitch in your delivery. I've seen pitchers deliver fastballs that were hard and accurate even though they may have accidentally fallen off to one side of the mound, or stepped a bit off. There is not much chance to correct your delivery when you're throwing a knuckleball.

Here's the correct pitching motion, from set to release (shown for a right-handed pitcher).

Start with the balls of your feet on the front edge of the rubber, facing straight toward the target.

Step back without shifting your weight, almost past your heel, with the foot opposite your pitching hand.

The set (left) and the step back (right), as seen by the catcher:

Next, as seen from third base:

Left: The pitcher has pivoted to the right, body facing third base. The front knee has been lifted straight up, and the stride foot is now starting to turn toward the target and move forward and down as the pitching hand breaks from the glove. The shoulder blades are pinched together by now.

Right: The stride foot has been planted, the pitching

hand is straight up, the hips and shoulders have not yet turned toward the target.

Left: The hips are turned toward the target, the rear foot is turning over on the top of the toes and is about to be pulled from the rubber, and the shoulders have not turned toward the target quite yet.

Center: The hips and shoulders are square to the target, the elbow has led the forearm and hand forward, and the forearm is swinging forward with a stiff wrist. The elbow should ideally be level with the shoulder. *All your velocity should be generated by the time your elbow is even with the side of your body.* You may elect to use the last few inches of your delivery before release to concentrate on the feel of the ball and accuracy.

Right: The ball has been released, the wrist finally breaks, and the pitcher follows through generally forward and remaining vertical. The shoulders may rotate a little further from here.

As you can see, there are differences between the standard fastball power-pitching positions and those of a knuckleball pitcher. Most other pitchers use a longer stride, so as not to lose balance—maybe about 60 percent of their height. Also, knuckleball pitchers generally finish pretty much vertical, with little follow-through, and release the ball on a slightly upward arc, though some do release it farther forward and with a longer stride, closer to the form of regular pitchers.

One interesting trait you may develop: strong fingers. Some pitchers report that they feel like they're tapping their fingertips straight into the back of the ball on release. This repetitive motion may strengthen those fingers and help develop a consistent forward low-rotation delivery. Will exercise help? Not as much as practicing a lot.

· 4 ·

Advanced Techniques, Q & A

Learning to throw knuckleballs is like learning to throw darts at a bull's-eye: ten minutes to teach but a lifetime to learn. Longtime knuckleball pitchers agree with me to a man. It's hard to believe that you keep on learning what you can and should do with what looks like a simple pitch, long after you learned to throw good ones, but it's true. It seems that no matter what your level of mastery of the pitch, you never trust it completely, so the knuckleball community is a tight-knit group, constantly swapping observations and suggestions among themselves. Most of the following have come from the message board on www.knuckleballhq.com.

Q: If it's so easy on the arm, why doesn't everyone throw it?

A: Tim Kurkjian of CNNSI once asked Charlie Hough why more pitchers didn't throw a knuckleball. Hough shot back: "Why don't more pitchers throw 95 miles per hour? Because it's really hard to do!"

Q: All I have to do is learn this trick pitch and I'm in the major leagues, right?

A: Sorry, but no. The biggest mistake many beginners make is to consider themselves knuckleball pitchers. They think they can do anything on the mound because they have a trick pitch, like something from a Bugs Bunny cartoon or a carnival sideshow. Of all the advanced knuckleball pitchers I've ever talked with, none say there's any truth to that. But they all appreciate the idea that you want to fool batters.

Something may happen in a game that may lead you to believe you have an easy magic trick, but don't be fooled. Things will change. Charlie Zink once threw a knuckleball to a batter who swung so hard he pulled a muscle and had to be taken out of the game. Charlie had a good laugh out of it, but the incident probably forced the other batters to settle down and be patient, and *patient batters can be a knuckleball pitcher's toughest challenge.*

To throw a knuckleball and win, you have to consider yourself a pitcher who throws a knuckleball, not a knuckleball pitcher, even though you may be called a knuckleball pitcher. You have to do many of the same things a successful pitcher does. Throwing a knuckleball not only won't fix any pitching problems you may have, it will force you to think a little differently on the mound.

Remember the cornerstones of any pitching plan? Throw strikes, mix speeds, and keep the ball down. If you throw mostly knuckleballs, what do you still have to do? All of the above. Unlike a regular pitcher, you can't throw knuckleballs to spots very reliably. So you need another approach to pitching, just as smart as any pitcher who does well by deception with conventional pitches.

Q: My knuckler goes all over the place, but my coach won't let me throw it.

A: In my many years of watching pitchers at various levels, the number one problem I see is not being able to throw strikes. It's not the best idea to throw all strikes, because if the batters realize this, they're more ready to swing, and you won't be able to fool them with something outside. Part of pitching is to make the batter think a pitch is a strike when it's a ball, and a ball when it's a strike. It's called expanding the strike zone. If a batter is willing to swing at offerings outside the strike zone, you have more places to put your next pitches, and it's harder to hit the ball. I saw one high schooler who threw in the 90s and was drafted very high by a major league team. My nephew thought that was pretty funny because his team could beat this guy just by watching and waiting and drawing walks—because he had a hard time throwing strikes.

It's common knowledge that knuckleball pitchers have a special difficulty in throwing strikes, if they haven't fine-tuned their delivery to keep the ball consistently around the strike zone. This has given the knuckleball a poor reputation in some baseball circles. But with proper pitching it often goes for a strike, and then it's quite a weapon.

If you can't throw strikes with a fastball, then don't bother throwing a pitch that can wander all over the place all by itself. You'll just add to your problem.

If throwing strikes is the real issue, maybe you can get an assistant coach to watch you in your side sessions, and maybe he'll convince your coach you deserve to use the knuckleball in a game. Most ballplayers at any level have another league or program available to pitch in, if the coach on your usual team won't let you throw it.

Q: I'm afraid to throw a pitch that slow. Batters will just wait for it and crush it.

A: This fear should not affect any pitcher who throws and understands breaking pitches: mixing speeds well. Warren Spahn said that batting is timing and pitching is upsetting timing. More pitchers at all levels need to understand that. It's an easy thing for most anyone to do, but many pitchers don't seem to have the confidence to change pace, thinking a slower pitch will get crushed. Maybe if they took a lot more batting practice, they'd understand how hard it is to shift mental gears and hit a surprise slow pitch when it's least expected.

Here's something worth careful observation: Do most opposing batters swing slightly downward on every pitch? If so, then consider the magic of the slope of the pitch. When major league baseball lowered the mound just a few inches some years back, pitching ERAs went up a few points. Pitches were more level with the batter and therefore easier to hit. Some major league teams have gotten the bright idea to make up for the leveling by trying to develop tall pitchers, and there is some practical sense to that. Swinging along the slope the ball comes in on is an effective way to hit it; a knuckleballer throwing a lot of stuff that comes in on a steep angle makes him appear to be three feet taller! This is no guarantee of success, however, especially if batters adjust by using an uppercut swing. Changing timing and ensuring that the ball has some side-to-side shift will greatly counteract that.

Q: I don't want to throw any pitch in the middle of the strike zone. So how do I control a knuckleball?

A: A knuckleball is a breaking pitch, so, like any other, you shouldn't throw many in the heart of the strike zone. It usually sinks, so it's generally best to throw it so it sinks and crosses the plate low in the strike zone. It's generally not a good idea to throw it high, because batters usually miss underneath pitches high in the strike zone, so you don't want to throw a pitch that might sink down and meet the bat! Note I say *generally*. These are not hard-and-fast rules. If you understand the situation and are pretty sure you can sneak one right down the heart of the plate, or throw one high, then go for it.

It's said that the batter tells you what to throw. Understanding the situation, knowing what will work next, and throwing it is the best way to pitch. Some youngsters get the idea they might want to try mixing in one pitch or another; if situations call for other pitches, then throw them. It's not exactly a good move to decide ahead of time that you'll throw a certain percentage of one kind of pitch or throw a pattern; let the situation determine it.

It's always good to feel confident in your knuckleball so you're pretty sure it will sink a lot (probably if you can throw it very slow to begin with); then you might get away with throwing one high in the zone. The batter may see this tempting slow pitch coming in high enough to see well, but he'll be fooled at the last moment when it sinks way below his bat. Little Leaguers are famous for going after high pitches, so you may do well at that level by throwing real slow ones high that they'll actually swing over.

Q: What about the hitter's saying, "If it's low, let it go; if it's high, let it fly"?

A: That doesn't work so well if the pitch ends up in the middle of the strike zone by complete surprise. I once saw a young batter who was unable to hit anything there, so he got a steady diet of anything and everything right down what normally is Home Run Alley. But usually keep the knuckleball out of the heart of the strike zone, just like any breaking pitch. Let the situation tell you what to throw, but a good mix lets you get away with something down the middle.

SECRET: Phil Niekro says the pitcher should throw the knuckleball to zones. There are three zones: low, middle, and high.

Open your hand wide with thumb down. That's the height of the bottom and top zones. Everything in the middle is where most of your pitches should avoid going. Regular pitchers work the "L"—the bottom edge and the inside edge on each batter. Knuckleball pitchers have to use the zones, but that's pretty simple.

First-pitch strikes can go anywhere, even in the middle zone. Almost every batter will give the first one to you, so make that first strike. From there, throw about 90 percent of your pitches in the low zone and about 10 percent in the top zone. (Once in a while you can throw anything you have in the middle zone, especially if you know the batter isn't expecting it.) You can throw hard knucklers in the low zone to disguise your other pitches. Low is where you need to mix speeds most, because that's where most of your pitches will end up.

Some pitchers become frustrated and throw harder knuckleballs, but remember *location*. If you throw them to the same target point, they'll not sink as much, and maybe will end up in that middle zone. Like *any* pitches, it's where they end up that counts. Using this plan, you can adjust to the good and not-so-good batters, use one pitch to set up the next one, and throw much like Greg Maddux. Not overpowering, just confusing.

Q: How can a knuckleball pitcher suddenly start to lose it on the mound?

A: A knuckleball pitcher's worst enemy is probably losing focus. Lose focus and you may throw one that rotates a little too much, or a lot of them, or you'll start to get more pitches up in the middle zone. It doesn't take much rotation to turn a knuckleball into a slowly rotating batting-practice fastball, and those pitches not only don't move side to side, they don't sink, and they're the ones that get hammered out of the park. I'll say more about that later.

Any pitcher should have strong mechanics and should work on agility, balance, and control, but it's especially important for a knuckleball pitcher. You've probably seen at least one get into trouble because he gave up a walk or two, a wild pitch or two, and maybe one long ball hit off a pitch that didn't do anything. Knuckleball pitchers, more than others, need to throw exactly the same way, over and over again. Other pitchers can get away with losing their balance slightly and throwing a slightly awkward pitch now and then. Knuckleball pitchers can't, because each pitch is more likely to be a ball. You may throw most of your knuckleballs with very slight rotation, but one with a little more than half a rotation (which is not much at all) will probably not do anything except get hit hard. If you lose focus, you won't throw knuckleballs with less spin; you'll throw them with just a little more spin, and that's dangerous. An indicator is solid hits off your pitches. This may come from having a little too much rotation on the ball, and that may be caused by releasing the ball in front of your normal release point, which is common when a pitcher is fatigued and losing focus.

Phil Niekro, on Tim Wakefield's early troubles: "Tim was so successful early, and then he just lost it. That's when it becomes very tough mentally to throw a pitch that everybody knows is coming. I've told him that he's got to keep learning, he's got to eat, sleep, walk, and talk the knuckleball until it floats in his bloodstream like a spirit inside him."

In his last few spring training outings in 1987, Joe Niekro said, "The way I judge my knuckleball is by what the batters are doing with it. If they're hitting line drives over the shortstop or hitting the ball out, it's pretty obvious it's not moving. There were maybe three line drives and the rest were worm-beaters that either did or didn't get out of the infield. That's when I know my knuckleball is moving, and it has been my last couple of times out."

Dennis Springer said, "You live and die with it, and hopefully, you don't die too much."

Q: How does a rookie at these knuckleballs try some in a game?

A: There are three kinds of knuckleball pitchers:

Some throw one when they're ahead in the count, or if the batter is swinging wildly at most anything thrown up there, no matter what the level or experience. This is a good way to start off. Most teams will have one pitcher who will air one out once in a while. Most junkball pitchers will try a few.

Other pitchers throw a high percentage of knuckleballs and get a lot of wild swinging strikes and a few more walks than most pitchers. The batters don't really know how to adjust, and they get impatient, seeing those big juicy pitches floating in. When they see pitches that are especially wild, they may lay off and get a free pass, but their first urge is to swing at all those grapefruits.

The elite pitchers have gone through a stretch where batters have discovered that very few of those knuckleballs are actually strikes, so they've learned to be patient. They either walk or wait for a genuine fat one to crush. These pitchers have to adjust by mixing speeds and heights, and by throwing an average number of strikes—numbers pretty reflective of a pitcher like Greg Maddux:

not overpowering and racking up the strikeouts, but drawing bad swings and getting a lot of badly hit balls.

A smart, experienced, and well-practiced knuckleball pitcher can throw one anytime, on any count, even when he needs a strike. Any pitcher who can throw any pitch he has anytime on any count is headed for the Hall of Fame.

Q: My kids face a Barry Bonds type. How can they beat this guy?

A: A sports magazine once published a photo of Bonds at bat, showing his strike zone and the pitch locations of the last ten home runs he hit. Most were well within that dangerous middle zone. A strike zone is *the* prime real estate in this game, so like actual real estate, the number one rule is location, location, location.

Phillies reliever Todd Jones: "Hitters tell me if they know *what* pitch is coming, they will lose their discipline in the strike zone and swing at anything. But when a hitter knows location, the pitcher basically is screwed."

If the pitch may sink a few inches or over a foot, plus maybe move left or right or both a few inches or a foot, no one can predict where that pitch will end up except by long-shot blind luck. Some good batters hit it well only because they know how to wait on it and carefully track it on the way in, then hit it along the slope it crosses the plate, which is an uppercut swing. For most batters, that's a tall order. Smart ones will adjust, though, so be ready to adjust.

Q: I'm afraid that if I throw a lot of knuckleballs, batters will catch up to them.

A: Skilled college batters can catch up to major league heat, because whacking a straight fastball is only a matter of timing. How does one "catch up" to a pitch that may come in slow or fast and wind up who knows where? One interesting note I've heard from a couple of highly skilled knuckleball pitchers: they usually throw with very little or almost no spin on the ball, throwing quite a few that move once or twice in big arcs from side to side, with a hard sink at the end. If they throw harder, perhaps in the mid-70s or more, the ball has a little more spin but enough to produce a different kind of movement. It doesn't move as much, but it may jump or hop or cut in a few different directions, then maybe not sink as much. This pitch is easier to throw for a strike but may be no easier to hit. Naturally you're closer to the point of putting too much rotation on the ball if you throw it hard, but if you have skill, focus, and confidence, you can throw as many of those as you want.

Q: You say it helps to mix speeds and arm slots, but I can't do that.

A: What are you talking about? You already do, and I'll prove it.

You fire low and hard to first on your pickoffs, right? And you throw high and easy lobs to your catcher on an intentional walk, right? So how can it be difficult to do the same thing when you throw pitches at the strike zone?

Most batters can tell the difference between two pitches that are thrown just a few miles per hour apart, and make the adjustment. The greater the difference between a few of your fastest pitches and a few of your slowest ones, the more likely you'll do well. Some pitchers think of this as having two different speed pitches, or three. Or more. Smart pitchers don't get hung up on individual numbers. They pitch a wide range of speeds. If you throw your fastball at, say, 80, and your breaking pitch at 70, you can do better by more mixing of the speeds in between. Pedro Martinez can throw only a few pitches, but at most any speed he wants, from the low 90s to the low 70s. The most successful pitchers often throw in a range going as low as about 80 percent of their fastest pitches. So if you throw around 90, you should also throw something as low as 18 miles per hour slower, or around the low 70s. If you watch pitchers closely at your level, you can easily tell when they shift gears and change speeds even a little. *Changing speeds over a wide range is an easy way to cover for the few pitches that don't go where you want or do what you want, no matter what you're throwing.*

Charlie Zink has an unusual weapon for most knuckleball pitchers: he can throw in the 60s as well as near 90. Charlie developed his hard fastball when young, so he's able to mix speeds on his knuckler as well as his other pitches. As you reach the age and level where you may be scouted by college or major league scouts, there is a giant difference between topping out in the 70s and in the 80s. Even major league batters see a lot of pitches in the 80s, but if you can't even reach that speed, your chances of reaching the next level drop considerably. You do have a very real shot at going to the next level, however, if you can show how crafty you can be, even if you don't have the heat of the gods.

Here's a secret: Smart scouts use their radar guns not just to see a pitcher's fastest gas, but his range of speeds. It's fairly easy to judge a pitch in the 70s or less, but it's hard to judge one in the 90s without a gun. Good scouts want to see that range and see mastery of it.

Once you're able to mix speeds and select your pitches well and put them where you want, the only thing holding you back is confidence. Tom Candiotti says, "The more weapons you have, the easier your job will be." Mixing speeds is an underused but highly effective weapon that knuckleball pitchers find easier to use than most pitchers—because they often have more confidence. They need confidence to make it anywhere, but even though that's more obvious in knuckleball pitchers, it's something any pitcher can use.

A SECRET FOR ROOKIES: If you want to throw just a few knuckleballs, or you're working on a different speed pitch, you may decide to throw one when it's okay to throw a junk pitch, such as when you're ahead in the count. If it doesn't do much, you'll probably not only be okay, you'll definitely give the batter something confusing to think about. To throw the knuckleball effectively, you have to throw it a lot, but even a bad one once in a while at the right time should work for you. Don't worry about a situation where you want to try something new that you're not sure of. You always know what's coming before the batter does, right? So you should be always one step ahead of him. Think of yourself as a magician showing a

pretty lame trick—lame to you, but the crowd loves it and
it works, so you keep it in the act. Because of that, I advo-
cate throwing either fewer than 10 percent or more than
80 percent knuckleballs in a game. If you throw almost all
knuckleballs, just remember that if they're not working
for you, you'd better have other pitches you can depend
on.

Q: I heard the knuckleball relies on breezes and air
currents, and that may make it hard to throw for strikes.

A: Correct, upsetting as it may be to the inexperienced. Skilled pitchers adjust for it. They notice theirs is
different if thrown into the wind. Understand that when
throwing into a wind, the airspeed of the ball and the
speed toward the plate are two different things. For example, if the wind is 70 miles per hour in your face and you
throw the ball with an airspeed of 70, it will drop straight
down. A wind of 70 at your back and throwing it at 70 will
get it across the plate in a blink! Think about this: when
we mention the speed of the pitch, we assume the air is
still. Throwing a knuckleball around 70 (ground speed)
into a wind of 20 means you actually threw it into the wind
at 90. The faster a knuckleball goes through the air, the
more it's held in line by the airflow and the less it will
move from side to side. It may not sink as much, either.
Most knuckleball pitchers like to throw into a light,
steady breeze. That way they can throw more easily and
concentrate on throwing the pitch where they want it and
keeping the spin down. (You can also picture the arm
movement that goes with these pitches, and how that may

help fool batters who are looking for a particular speed.) A strong wind makes it harder, because they have to throw it hard enough to get it to the plate. They may solve this by throwing it higher, so it has more arc, which will help get it there and help cover for any lack of movement it may have. A batter may like the wind going out, but in most cases it's a knuckleball pitcher's friend. Naturally, a knuckleball is harder to control in a strong crosswind, too, so you have to adjust by waiting for it to die down, more so than most other pitchers. Obviously it takes experience and bravery to make those adjustments.

Daniel (Danny) Boone, on his famous namesake ancestor: "I don't know if he'd have had the courage to throw a knuckleball on a 3-2 count with the bases loaded."

Q: So how can I tell if it's the knuckleball, or if it's me doing good or bad?

A: It takes unusual (but not difficult) awareness of your pitching to recognize what you're doing right and wrong, and if things may change for better or worse. If you give up a hit, you have to know why. Was it just good batting, or were you not pitching as well as you should? This goes for *any* pitcher. Depend on your catcher to keep you informed.

Hoyt Wilhelm: "You can throw a bad one once in a while if you're throwing a lot of good ones. But you can't throw two or three bad ones in a row. Sometimes when I go out there I throw just about every one of them good. At other times it's just nothing. And I get hit. It takes a lot of work and a lot of concentration. It's that delicate a pitch."

Your catcher sees it all, up close and personal. A pitcher's entire focus is on what happens in and around the strike zone, but that's many feet away from you and hard to see. Your catcher not only sees all and can judge right down to an inch, he has to react to anything that surprises him. Just how he's catching your pitches ought to be enough to tell you most everything you need to know, but whether the ball has effective movement is something he has to communicate well to you. If you're suddenly putting too much spin on it and it therefore looks very hittable, he knows it immediately, and he has to let you know quickly what it's doing wrong.

Q: Tom Candiotti says not to drop down to the side during your delivery: you'll lose your release point.

A: You might be doing that already in throwing your pickoffs.

Understand what you need to do when you pitch. Film yourself from the side and notice that you release the ball in the exact same place vertically, in relation to your body, face, and head, every time. If you drop down and throw more sidearm, the ball tends to sail across your body and to the other side. If you try just one submarine pitch, it may really sail. That's because you're losing your release point. *The more you drop your arm, the natural tendency is to release farther ahead and across your body.*

The diagram on the next page shows the strike zone as the pitcher would be looking at it. A right-handed pitcher throwing three-quarters might have an arm angle that follows a line like A-B through the strike zone. Sidearm, F-E; submarine, D-C. For a lefty, it's C-D, E-F, B-A. Like throwing darts, it's easier to throw accurately the closer your throw is to the level of your eyes and nearer your head. Release late for a righty and you'll throw toward B, E, and C. For a lefty, it's D, F, and A.

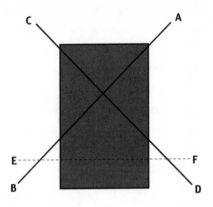

How to counteract that? Note where you release on the video, and *always* release when you reach a line drawn vertically down from that point.

The more you release in front of this line, the more the ball will sail across the strike zone toward the other side. You'll feel like you're releasing early, but if you're on the line, you'll release pretty much correctly. Just remember that the farther you drop your arm, the harder it is to generate velocity and throw accurately.

One extremely useful reason why you should at least be comfortable with dropping down to the side is when you have men on base. Phil Niekro had a *great* pickoff move, in part because he naturally threw at a low three-quarters angle, almost sidearm. He never had to pick his arm up much from the set position in order to fire a fastball to first. If you throw mostly knuckleballs, you're much less likely to hurt yourself when you throw a few of *anything* sidearm, as opposed to a fastball-firing power pitcher.

HOT TIP: Being able to pitch in a low three-quarters slot will help prevent steals because base runners won't think you're slow to the plate. You'll have little extra movement, and it's extra movement that takes time, time that base-stealers find useful.

Another reason for dropping down is that if you want to throw to a zone, low, high, or in the middle, it may be easier to throw across the zone you want to throw to. That way you may miss left or right but still on the correct level. Just understand that a batter may recognize this and get a feel for how high the pitch may be—but the wandering of a knuckleball will help counteract that. Understand the principle of pitch location: it's best to work the bottom edge and the inside edge of the strike zone, assuming you're throwing a locatable pitch. With a knuckleball, you may decide to throw it so you'll have the greatest margin for error if you miss, or if it flattens out on you. Having a pretty good guess what the batter may do is always helpful, no matter what you throw. But you won't have to constantly think about where the batter likes it or where he can't hit it nearly as much as a regular pitcher will.

Q: Some pitchers report they can actually locate their knuckleball.

A: Sometimes, yes. A few have figured out how to release with a last-moment twist of the wrist, like turning a doorknob, producing a light rotation that makes the ball spiral, or corkscrew, if they manage to pull it off. It sounds like only Bugs Bunny can do this, but I've thrown one, and others have thrown a few, with not a lot of consistency, but most hope to achieve this Holy Grail of knuckleballs. R. A. Dickey of the Texas Rangers throws one he calls the "Thing." He describes it as a cross between a splitter and a knuckle-curve, but this explains the action, not necessarily the grip or release. It is a true locatable knuckleball, a killer pitch that sinks and cuts right. You might be able to duplicate it by running your thumb along a seam and gripping a little low of center, so that when you release, the ball rolls forward out of your hand and your thumb holds it back ever so slightly. The pitch has a light forward rotation and slight rotation to the side opposite the thumb. Its angle of travel will depend on your arm slot, as most breaking pitches do. Other pitchers have experimented with grips that produce a very light rotation and subsequent drift to one side, with or without a lot of sink. Anyone mastering such a pitch may be headed for the Hall of Fame, and this is definitely possible for anyone who understands what he's doing, who has skill, and who experiments with grips and deliveries.

One semi-pro pitcher reports he's developed the mechanics to throw a knuckleball consistently with last-moment explosive movement. His numbers are definitely above average, so he's obviously not doing anything to walk more batters or produce any laughable stats. Here is how he does it—but understand that this is much like making a helicopter hover, it takes balance and the coordination of several controls to succeed. You can't just read about it in a book and do it right away. It requires delicate feel and consistent mechanics to accomplish.

I call one part of this the "spider on the wall." Place your fingertips on a wall in front of you so that your hand looks like a spider. Notice what fingertip is up. Notice you can rotate your hand so any of your fingers will be uppermost. Unlike other pitches that demand you have particular fingers at a particular clock position on release, you may find that releasing the knuckleball with a particular finger up will produce the action you want. You can also turn your hand palm out or palm in at release to get the movement you want. You may also find that rotating your hand from one position to another at the very last moment may take away the last little bit of spin, or launch the ball with the seams positioned in such a way that you get a consistent controllable action.

Remember the photo of the ball rotated just 15 degrees? Now you know just how delicate this can be and why I suggest that you mix speeds to confuse batters. This hand placement takes a strong awareness of how the ball rotates out of your hand. A slight change in how the seams are oriented in your hand will change all that too. So will your velocity. *All this is extremely hard and rare to do.* You have to practice a lot ever to hope to throw this way with any consistency. That's why I suggest changing speeds to throw effectively: it's far easier to do.

Q: I heard about a minor league pitcher who hoped to get a lot of lessons from Tim Wakefield, but didn't. I thought knuckleball pitchers like to get together and swap tips?

A: This goes back to a question I once posed to Wilbur Wood. I asked him if he treated the knuckleball like a class of pitches, sort of an assortment of different types. He said, "I tried to." Modest words from a guy who had more to show about this pitch than almost anyone realized. Some pitchers like Bobby Shantz do well using a knuckleball as a strike-three changeup and never bother doing anything else. Some throw a lot of easy lollipops and get outs, inning after inning. Some throw a big mix of speeds and deliveries and make a career that way. Sure, knuckleball pitchers find each other like two bears in the tundra, then get together to swap ideas and suggestions. But when it comes to getting a never-fail recipe for winning, there is none. If there were one for conventional pitchers, each major league team would have three future

Hall of Famers on its staff. Knuckleballs are tougher to throw.

If you think about all the different grips and deliveries and ways you can succeed if you experiment yourself, all the pitches that could be in your bag of tricks that are just different-flavor knuckleballs, you'll fully realize that no one can tell you how to throw *your* individual knuckleball and get the outs you want. You're still a pitcher who just happens to throw knuckleballs. Pitching is so complicated that no one can give you one hot, surefire tip that's guaranteed to help. No one knows what you need to know or everything you already know. Your skills, your style, the situations you face—all are highly individual and something you have to work out yourself. Former Red Sox catcher Rich Gedman said, "You train yourself. You have to teach yourself the things you need to succeed. Others can give you ideas, but you have to pick and choose and find what works for you." I'm sure he was talking about many things besides catching.

Q: Does it take a special physical makeup to throw knuckleballs?

A: Unlike power pitching, you don't need a special physical makeup to be able to throw world-class knuckleballs over and over again. But what it does take is brains. Hoyt Wilhelm told me something very useful to anyone throwing knuckleballs or thinking about it: "You gotta be smart to throw them." Anyone winning in the major leagues with a pitch with junior-high velocity has to be whip-smart.

Q: So do any knuckleball pitchers disagree?

A: Yes, but only because they may have seen an aspect of the pitch that works for them, and so they feel you need that element to succeed. One example: I suggested the possibility of dropping down to the side to Tom Candiotti, and he said, "No! You'll lose your release point!" He was pretty emphatic about it. I understand why he said that. Most knuckleball pitchers can't drop down to the side and throw an effective pitch. The point of this book, however, is to show that *a few* pitchers can add that delivery to their bag of tricks, *a few* can throw a lot of hard ones, *a few* do well digging their nails into the seams. I offer you a wide range of possibilities; pick and choose to make your pitch work. Don't think you need to do everything here to succeed, or even many different things, and don't think you should try a second type of knuckleball or delivery until you've mastered one (unless you find something isn't working at all). Candiotti was exactly right when he said to try to have as many things in your bag of tricks as you can—*but they all must work for you!* So if you truly can't drop down to the side with any reliability, try something you *can* do.

Jim Bouton sums it up best: "You need the fingers of a safecracker and the mind of a Zen Buddhist to throw it."

Q: Your explanation of the physics of it was disputed by an aerodynamics professor. Why?

A: He disagreed with it. I say up front that I explain the knuckleball so the layman can get a feel for why it floats as it does. Even physics professors disagree on how

it works! They should know. They do the measurements
and run the wind-tunnel tests and see the same numbers.
This is like a family squabble, a domestic dispute among
people you'd think would automatically love one another,
and I'm avoiding it.

Q: You say you shouldn't add a knuckleball to your bag
of tricks unless it works for you, but you say it's okay to
throw a few iffy ones in a game. Can you explain that?

A: Great question. The answer has to do with basic
pitching. You can throw a few of any pitch you want to try
and not consider it to be part of your bag. You can throw
junk pitches or one you're working on as maybe a first-
pitch strike, or, more likely, on a count when you can
waste one, such as 0-2 or 1-2, with not much to be concerned about otherwise. The one you have in your bag of
tricks is a decent pitch on its own, one you already com-
mand, one you won't mind breaking out a dozen times or
more in a game, one that may cross up the batter on its
own, one you may throw back-to-back, one you may consider your regular No. 1, No. 2, or No. 3 pitch, or one you
can use as an out pitch.

· 5 ·

How to Hit It

Richie Hebner: "Hitting Niekro's knuckleball is like eating soup with a fork."

Former coach Tim Owens: "The knuckleball screws up the mind."

Tim McCarver: "Hitting that thing is like trying to catch a butterfly with a pair of tweezers."

Rick Monday, to Phil Niekro: "When I swing, don't laugh. It giggles as it goes by."

Randy Hundley's take on it: "You see the ball and you just know you've got a bead on it, then you swing, and poof, it's not there anymore."

Bobby Murcer, on Phil Niekro: "Trying to hit Phil Niekro is like trying to eat Jell-o with chopsticks. Sometimes you get a piece, but most of the time you get hungry."

Willie Stargell calls the knuckleball "a butterfly with hiccups."

Floyd Robinson reportedly swung at one that went *behind* him.

I was told I should sell these secrets for a million dollars, but I won't, for one reason: what I offer you here are suggestions to improve your chances of hitting knuckleballs, but they aren't surefire. What is certain, however, is that I'll disprove an old wives' tale or two.

First, understand that knuckleballs don't do anything different just because they're thrown lefty or righty, or three-quarters or sidearm. In fact, a pitcher who throws at least two different speed knuckleballs may be able to confuse batters by throwing them from a different arm angle. So, if you're a hitter, don't treat knuckleballs as a new class of magic trick. You might give the pitcher a mental edge. If you have never seen a knuckleball, or just a few, you're probably not ready to hit one. Some major league batters openly admit that they just go up to the plate and not think about hitting a knuckleball, because it might mess up their swing for days.

John Kruk, on hitting a knuckleball: "I'd rather have my leg cut off than do that all day. You just hope it hits your bat in a good spot."

And Dick Allen: "I never worry about it. I just take my three swings and go sit on the bench. I'm afraid if I ever think about hitting it, I'll mess up my swing for life."

And the greatest hitter of all time, Pete Rose: "I work for three weeks to get my swing down pat and Phil [Niekro] messes it up in one night. . . . Trying to hit that thing is a miserable way to make a living."

Ernie Banks, on Phil Niekro: "He simply destroys your timing with that knuckleball. It comes flying in there dipping and hopping like crazy, and you just can't hit it."

Because knuckleballs are no different from either side, knuckleball pitchers aren't subject to the late-inning, tight-score, lefty-righty double switch. So if you see one early in the game and he's doing at all well, you're more likely to see him through the entire game. Uh-oh.

So how do you improve your odds of hitting the knuckler? Well, one thing you might try is to move up in the batter's box. Try to be close to the pitch before it breaks. Knuckleballs may break in any direction, move a little or a lot, and may sink a lot or a little—all at any time. If the pitcher is not throwing many that end up low, by all means move up in the box and try to get them when they're still up in the strike zone. It's said that in each at-bat the hitter gets one good pitch to hit. Moving up in the box may give you one higher in the zone, good enough to crush.

Another thing you should do is to wait on them. Knuckleballs are slower pitches. Wait, wait, wait. If someone hits one hard, chances are good that it will be pulled down the line and foul, because most batters aren't used to having to wait so long. They're way ahead of it.

As a hitter, you may like the wind blowing out, but a sharp knuckleball pitcher knows he can throw it easier through a wind that will help it dance, so be alert, and don't think it'll be easy to hit one out. You'll have more problems connecting with that pitch!

The knuckleball is also a sinker pitch, maybe a hard sinker, so it's best to try to hit it along the same angle it's coming in on, and drive it straight back in that direction, which means you'll probably do better with a slight upper-cut swing. The lower his arm angle, the harder time a pitcher has controlling the pitch and generating velocity. But this principle works both ways. The farther down and away the pitch is from the batter's eyes, the harder it is to hit the ball square and with power, especially if it comes in on the same angle as one thrown from a higher arm slot. Try to find the angle it will be coming in on when it arrives.

To maintain control, concentrate on making contact. You might do better by cutting down on your swing. I saw a picture of Reggie Jackson who had obviously been tempted by a knuckleball from Phil Niekro. He not only missed, he swung so hard he almost screwed himself into the ground. If you understand physics and you understand the ideal launch angle of a batted ball, you'll understand that if you can hit a ball square, and if it's coming in at an angle close to the ideal home run launch angle of about 40 degrees, your chances of hitting it deep are good without the need for a long and powerful swing. A foot past the fence is good enough. So think "wait," then "quick and compact." And if the ball doesn't flutter, you're swinging at a batting-practice fastball. Unfortunately, this approach isn't perfect, because you may hit one just like that and it will be an easy fly-ball out.

The sweet spot on a wooden bat is about seven to eight inches down from the head; on an aluminum bat it's about there, only longer. You can swing at a pitch from about waist-high up with a level swing and maybe still hit it on the sweet spot if it doesn't move too much right or left, or too late for you to adjust. Around knee level your bat is tilted, reducing your margin of error. Waiting, having a quick bat, and swinging for solid contact will help. Also remember that aluminum bats will be somewhat more effective on knuckleballs—but they're more effective on any pitch. If you aren't used to a wooden bat, you'll discover that your normal long swing developed from swinging aluminum is pretty ineffective, and may be especially useless on floaters.

If you've never experienced a knuckleball's slow arrival, you'll show it on your first swing. You'll probably buckle your knees, lean forward, and chop down on it, just trying to make contact. You won't hit it. You'll have to realize that the knuckleball will destroy your timing if you permit it to, so work on holding back, keeping your weight back, and taking a tight, compact, last-moment, slightly uppercut swing.

Next, you'll have to work on hitting it fair, and hitting it where it will fall for a hit. A big home run swing may result only in a long and easy fly ball, so recognize what adjustments you have to make in your swing to get the results you want. *Don't be tempted and overswing*. A 125-foot base hit is better than a 400-foot fly out.

Recent reports of locatable knuckleballs may spell deadly trouble for hitters. A few pitchers claim to have developed the ability to place just the lightest rotation on the ball so as to make it drift to one side or another with some reliability. Is this true? Well, the Hall of Fame is watching with interest. Considering the fact that it takes only a whisper of rotation to make a knuckleball do something entirely different, it remains to be seen if batters could pick this up and hit the pitch well, as they do by picking up the rotation of most other pitches. Picking up the grip and rotation out of the pitcher's hand will likely continue to be essentially useless when a butterfly pitcher is on the hill.

One last thing: knuckleball pitchers read this too.

· 6 ·

How to Catch It (Maybe)

On a live internet chat, a fan asked Jason Varitek: "Is it true that you can't catch a knuckleball? My friend said so, but I disagree."

"Well," Varitek replied, "I'd say that Wake has thrown over 3,000 knuckleballs and I know I've caught at least one of 'em."

Charlie Lau: "There are two theories on catching the knuckleball. Unfortunately, neither of them works."

A razor-sharp catcher like Varitek is in a better position to know a few little but highly effective things about catching the knuckleball that make him look like a wizard. I got these tips from him and a few others who have figured it out. Fortunately, knowing these tips makes the job a lot easier—but never easy. Varitek answers the question: How hard is it to catch them? "It's never relaxing, that's for sure. It's like snowflakes—no two are ever alike." To the credit of the Red Sox catching staff, Doug Mirabelli has taken over the duties of catching Tim Wakefield with equal success.

At first Varitek used a specially designed custom mitt that's large enough to corral those knucklers that take a last-moment wiggle. They're expensive, but the top knuckleball pitchers have at least one for their catcher. Others can go quite a long way to help their catcher by providing a softball first-baseman's mitt.

Many catchers like to hang their mitt out straight in front of them, but a huge mitt like this is heavy, forcing them to make an adjustment that may help them in another way. Sometimes they just hold the mitt back a little, so they can better handle the weight of it, and this allows them to shift it side to side at the last moment more easily. Like batters, catchers have timing, and it can be thrown off by pitches coming in very slow. So they too must wait on the pitch. Mirabelli has gone to a smaller mitt, which he probably found easier to shift to lasso those wild ones. Is all this about different size mitts conflicting advice? No, it's personal choice. Make yours.

It's a common habit to let your mitt or glove do most of the work, which is usually okay except when you're catching a ball that flutters. It helps to imagine that you don't have a mitt on; concentrate on catching it as if you were bare-handed. That gives you the extra width all around to help grab one that moves a little at the last moment.

So where do you put your other hand? One of two places: either behind you, or directly behind the mitt, *not* on the outside edge of the mitt. (That's asking for broken fingers!) Many prefer behind the mitt for two reasons: there is plenty of protection there, and the hand is more available for a quick throw to a base. The choice may come down to which way you normally catch that allows you to keep your balance and what you're comfortable with. An option is to place your other hand off to the side of the mitt a little, which allows you a quicker reach for the ball on a throw to a base, and may help your balance.

Because a knuckleball sinks at the last moment and may move quite a distance from side to side, holding the mitt closer to you allows you to tilt it upward more, making it much easier to catch the ball square. Crouching with your feet a couple of inches wider and turned slightly outward also helps you corral the sudden sinkers in the dirt, and helps you keep your balance if you have to shift one way or another at the last moment. Those last two words are probably your most important words to remember: "last moment." "You have to wait as long as possible, because it moves at the last moment," says Varitek. You can't worry about catching it until it gets to you, and you don't know what it will do when it gets to you, so you have to adjust so that you can be ready to make a last-moment stab at the ball.

Even the best catchers admit they have their problems catching the knuckleball. Bob Uecker was traded to the Braves for another catcher because the Braves saw him as better for Phil Niekro. Nevertheless, here is Uecker on the best way to catch it: "Wait'll it stops rolling, then go pick it up." And on the benefits of catching it: "I met a lot of important people. They all sit behind home plate."

No matter what kinds of knuckleballs you catch, you'll have to make some of these adjustments. You may have a pitcher who throws them with just a little shimmy and a little sink, making them more catchable and more locatable, and just a little different from what you're used to. No matter what, it's a giant help to catch at least one bullpen before game time and discuss with your pitcher your mutual game plan and his pitches. You can also consider setting up inside or outside, not only for a locatable pitch as you always do. Try a few setups if you're calling for the butterfly, if you think someone will pick up on them and guess wrong. Of course, be ready to catch that thing! You can get into a batter's head just as much as that strange pitch you have to catch.

Despite your best-laid plans, the unexpected will happen, maybe even for the best. Here's a play Bob Uecker remembers: "[Phil] Niekro struck out a hitter once, and I never touched the ball. It hit me in the shinguard, bounced out to Clete Boyer at third base, and he threw out the runner at first. Talk about a weird assist: 2-5-3 on a strikeout."

It's said that catcher's equipment are the tools of ignorance. While I'll be kinder, a knuckleball pitcher should regard any catcher who's enthusiastic for catching his dizzy deliveries as the best friend anyone could ever have.

· 7 ·

How to Coach It

It's an old baseball maxim: You don't want a knuckleballer for you or against you. When you think about how they can drive you nuts when they're throwing well for the other side, or giving up the universe when they're throwing lousy for you, this saying is all too true.

There are a few things to watch out for that will help you coach a knuckleballer and don't necessarily demand that you have any deep knowledge of the pitch itself. You'll probably recognize them as things you should watch for no matter who is on the mound and what pitches are being thrown.

First, the knuckleball is a breaking pitch, and like any other, it shouldn't be up in the strike zone except on rare occasions. From the dugout you should be able to tell if your pitcher is getting hit hard because he's getting too many up in the zone. You have a great angle to see that. It goes without saying that a pitch this slow and hard to catch may inspire base runners to steal, which may be the bigger problem. So it's smart for your pitcher and catcher to practice pickoffs, pitchouts, and throws down to second, and get better at them.

Second, you should be able to see the stitches almost as well as anyone behind the plate. If you're not seeing them and your pitcher is giving up a lot of solid line drives (or worse), he may be putting too much spin on the ball. With just a little practice, if he's on, you should be able to see his pitches consistently sink. If you don't see much sink, he's throwing batting practice, and you'd better recognize it *fast*.

Third, is your pitcher successful with a mix of pitches and speeds, and is he using them? Do you notice an unusual number of passed balls, wild pitches, or walks? A knuckleball can be controlled—not quite like anything else, but controlled nevertheless—and your team shouldn't be victimized by any pitcher who lacks control. *If your catcher has a feel for the pitch and knows how to run the game with a knuckleballer on the mound, he's the one to talk with.*

From there, it's your decision as to whether the pitcher comes out and when. If you're a decent coach, *you* decide whether he comes out or works through it. Sometimes just a visit to the mound is enough to get his focus back, if that's his problem. You'll have to know him and do what you need to, as you would with any other pitcher.

It's said that you can be as nervous as you want to be on the field, just don't ever show it. This may be especially true for anyone who throws a pitch that everyone knows is coming. Understand that, like any other pitch, if it's

reachable, the batter can get lucky and hit it. One, anyway. Because many knuckleballs are not hit well, or are
hit by sheer luck, you may be more concerned with your
pitcher getting outs than strikes. Many outs come from
weak pop-ups or easy ground balls because the knuckleball is so hard to hit square. You shouldn't blame a knuckleball pitcher if his fielders can't handle basic hit balls.

A pitcher may grow frustrated and start throwing
harder; if he does, and at the same spot, he may get
whacked around. He has to anticipate where the ball will
sink to. Hard ones won't sink so much, so in most cases
they have to be aimed at the bottom edge of the strike
zone. If he can't keep the knuckler down, he's no different
from any other pitcher who should keep breaking pitches
low in the zone to be effective.

If he's throwing a lot of slow ones and you see the batters using their golf clubs on it, he should immediately
throw harder ones, pounding the bottom edge of the zone.
There's a difference between a bad swing and an uppercut
home run swing. If you can't afford a long ball, he has to
flatten the batters' swings. Experienced knuckleballers
can throw them so they explode at the last moment,
which is an effective way to prevent hitters from using
those 5-wood shots to the fence. For most pitchers they're
harder to throw, but if your pitcher can throw a lot of them
in that situation, he should. His temptation is to continue throwing soft ones, but there may be a time when he
has to go after the hitters and attack the bottom of the
strike zone. He should work on the side to develop that
kind of knuckleball: you don't want it to float, you don't

want it to flutter. You want it to *explode*. If he can throw even a few of those and once in a while, it will make all his pitches dramatically better. I suggest mixing speeds and trying mostly lazy ones only because this wrecks most batters' timing. If he shows one kind too often, and the hitters are dialing in on it, he's got to give them a different look. Most likely he'll have to break out the mean stuff if you're in a league that has a book on pitchers. He should always be ready to stop playing nice!

Do I keep saying "him" for a reason? Only for convenience. The ladies are just as capable of throwing knuckleballs. Bill Lee's aunt, Annabelle (Lefty) Lee Harmon, threw the first perfect game in the All-American Girls Professional Baseball League, and would you care to guess what she threw? I realize what kind of pitcher most Little League teams want, but if you have a girl on your team who demonstrates an ability to throw knuckleballs and win with her pitching style, you'd be crazy not to let her take a shot at starting.

University of Miami pitcher Sean Flaherty told me about a game he once pitched. Apparently no one in the game had ever faced a knuckleball pitcher, especially a good one. The other high school team laughed at him in the first inning. By the third, the batters were getting coached from the stands. By the sixth, they were getting *angry and frustrated* coaching from everyone except Sean's team—which thoroughly enjoyed the proceedings. If you're going to face a knuckleball pitcher, you should prepare your batters in advance with a little BP against one, if that's possible.

In professional ball, the idea is to develop players for the next level, so I see little hope for a knuckleballer in his thirties or older signing on. Age does unusual things to knuckleball pitchers. It's said that they don't lose their velocity, even in the grave. That's only a slight exaggeration. Smart scouts and coaches, however, notice that other tools may be lacking because of age, and that alone may make the difference. As players, they still must at least hold their own on pickoffs, hitting, fielding, and running bases. As of this writing, Bill Downs, a forty-plus amateur, may yet be signed for reasons that have to do with the kinds of clubs he approaches: independent league teams. They like to fill seats, first and foremost, and if Bill can put on a show and get outs, his other possible shortcomings may be overlooked. Like any player, a knuckleball pitcher should be ready to show he's generally at least average—if not above—regardless of age. Charlie Hough said he had to retire because he couldn't cover first anymore.

You can get additional coaching and pitching tips, and follow the exploits of knuckleball pitchers the world over, by logging on to www.knuckleballhq.com, Knuckleball Headquarters, and clicking on the message board link. This is a discussion board open to view for anyone. Simply registering allows you to put in your two cents' worth.

Can you recognize an ideal mentality for a knuckleball pitcher? It's said that the best of them have an easy grasp of complex physical activities. Tim Wakefield has done calligraphy and piloted planes. Phil Niekro used to do the polka. Sean Flaherty is an accomplished musician on more than one instrument.

Positioning your players may be a complex activity of your own. Whether you have a potential Hall of Famer or a tryout on the mound, you should consider shifting your fielders to play the pull—maybe. Many batters will be way ahead of the slow knuckleball, and you may get a lot of screamers down the line.

Other coaches have found that a good knuckleball pitcher will give up an unusual number of off-field flares as well, so they might set up an odd shift: the second baseman or shortstop—whichever one is on the pull side—plays a few steps toward the line, center fielder the same, first or third baseman on that side a few steps toward the line and in a couple of steps (to help cut off doubles down the line). Infielders on the other side play a couple of steps toward their line, and the outfielder on that side a few steps toward that line and in a couple more steps than the fielder on the other line, to try to take away the dink off-field singles popped over the infield into no-man's land. This scheme ignores the deep shots, but many knuckleballers give up towering fly balls that are generally easy to track down even if the outfielders are a few steps out of normal position. As always, a smart coach will have a feel for how batters will react and place his fielders accordingly, but I'd advise against making blind, knee-jerk assumptions. One of the most effective batters on my son's team was a big lefty. How you shift for lefties was the exact wrong thing to do with this guy, because he was known to us as a power line-drive hitter who swung late and ripped drives down the third-base line. So anytime we saw fielders shift right for him, we shut up and enjoyed the results. Other coaches never caught on. With a knuckleballer who reliably gives up hit balls in a particular way, it's smart to shift fielders to counter that.

There's always a little deception you can attempt at your leisure that may enhance your unusual weapon on the mound. A pitcher beats the batter, not the bat, and that's with guile. Tim Wakefield sometimes moves to the left or right of the rubber, which may help a regular pitcher steer his next offering left or right in the strike zone, but that won't do much for a knuckleball pitcher—maybe. The move may indicate a locatable pitch on the way, and the batter may anticipate that. Then again, it may indicate an adjustment in the delivery of a forthcoming knuckleball. The batter doesn't know. Remember what Todd Jones said about batters swinging at a particular kind of pitch they think is coming next? If that can be planted in the mind of the hitter, all the better.

You can also use that deception by shifting your fielders to make the batter think a particular pitch is coming. And there's always your catcher's setup. Your catcher can set up inside or outside, and if the batter catches on somehow, well, it doesn't matter if he's about to see a knuckleball. Remember: you probably know a thing or two about what your pitcher may produce while the opposing batters will always have to guess. Standard fare is to flash fake signs they can "steal," but you can do that with any pitcher, and he can shake off fake signs from your catcher. A combination of all these devices may get into the batter's head, and you'll have psychology on your side.

Because the knuckleball is such a delicate pitch, I suggest daily side sessions for the pitcher of fifteen minutes or more, to work on control and to maintain feel and mechanics. With the little this pitch takes out of an arm, there's not much advantage to any days of complete rest, but there's a big advantage to throwing just a few minutes every day. Phil Niekro advises that, and it's hard to argue with a Hall of Famer.

Despite what many think, batters can adjust to knuckleballs and away from them pretty quickly. George Brett says that the idea of sandwiching a knuckleballer as a starter between two power pitchers is overrated, and the evidence bears that out. Once every batter has seen the knuckler the first time through the batting order, they may be ready to kill it the next. Anyone throwing them with some kind of pattern—whether it's location or velocity or mix with other pitches—should be ready to make an adjustment. Some batters can adjust within one at-bat, and it's assumed that some batters will swing at a bad pitch at times just to try to fool the pitcher into serving up one they really can drive. *So a knuckleball pitcher may have to adjust from one pass through the batting order to the next, or give the hitters a different look if he comes in to relieve a pitcher getting hit, or make a smart adjustment within an individual at-bat. Stay focused on why your knuckleball pitcher is doing well or is about to get in trouble, and be able to explain why.* When you think of it, this is no different from handling any other pitcher.

If you're facing a knuckleball pitcher, review the chapter on how to hit. Understand that knuckleball pitchers often have their own style. Maybe one throws harder than another, one mixes speeds better, and all of them have other pitches at the ready. If you think a four-seamer and a two-seamer look different, you may be stunned at the wide difference between even a lame four-seam fastball and a slow and wobbly knuckleball. Even rookie knuckleball pitchers often understand the importance of changing speeds from offering to offering, so your batters must work on being patient and having a quick, compact, contact swing to have much luck. I say "luck" because your batters may be used to predicting where other pitches may go and are used to the timing; but when a knuckleball comes in that may take an amazing twist and turn on the way, the usual "at least one pitch in every at-bat is yours to hit" doesn't apply unless they're better disciplined than usual.

An interesting aspect of this adjustment, depending on whose side the knuckleballer is on, is the long-term effect of learned plate discipline. If the batters adjust well, they may become better overall hitters when they face other pitchers. Good if they're batting for you, not so good if against you.

One useful weapon in a knuckleball pitcher's bag of tricks is having the smarts to think like any other pitcher, and finishing off a batter with high heat. Even in the major leagues, when the situation is right, *any* batter is susceptible to swinging at a hard one up and in. If major leaguers commonly fall victim to what seems like a lame trick, you may not be able to train it out of your batters, no matter what their level. And you can train your knuckleball pitcher to have a high hard one ready.

You may be intrigued to note a few other subtle traits of knuckleballers, which may leave you more or less concerned.

Most of them have shorter-than-usual strides, and they often stride the same all the time. Normal pitchers tend to shorten their strides when the mound is wet, which may cut their velocity and tend to bring the ball up in the strike zone. So, if your k-baller is pitching differently in the rain—better or worse—it may have nothing to do with a change in stride length.

The easy delivery may make it simple to incorporate a slide-step to help keep base runners close to the bag. The pitcher may decide to use a slide step consistently when throwing from the windup or from the stretch. Unlike most pitchers, he may find he can simplify his overall delivery this way. You surely already know that the simpler, the better. One rock-solid reliable element of his delivery will help you look elsewhere if a problem arises.

If your pitcher has insufficient velocity, he can lengthen his stride to approximate that of a regular pitcher. If he's also throwing too much up in the zone, he probably should be making more use of his legs, like any other pitcher. A longer stride may lower pitches in the zone, the opposite of shortening the stride. If he starts to hang his pitches, you can watch for that, but don't take the excuse that the pitch has a mind of its own. Any breaking pitch that hangs is there because the pitcher put it there.

Another trait of the knuckleballer you can watch for is how he's missing the strike zone. It's preferred to miss low more than inside or outside. Missing to the opposite side may indicate overthrowing, especially if he has an average three-quarter or low three-quarter arm slot. Also, low misses are more likely to be caught or stopped. Most professional hitters can pick up on the arm motion and have a pretty good idea of location, and they will assume this is no different for a knuckleball pitcher. Let's just say they may guess right a little less often about someone who throws a pitch that could wander a foot and a half left or right.

If your pitcher has been getting tagged lately, your first suggestion to him is to look at the speeds of his knucklers and the percentage of each. Batters may be keying on a particular speed. Try to find out if any batters you face are good high-ball or low-ball hitters, as with any other pitcher. Understand that slow knucklers may be most effective because of timing, but if the pitcher is depending on those and getting hit, faster pitches will give batters less time to adjust. Throwing at a speed the batter doesn't expect is one of the pitcher's strongest weapons and the one to keep uppermost in mind. Watch Tim Wakefield and you can see the magic of how a swarm of knuckleballs can mess up hitters' minds so badly that he can sneak in a fastball that's hardly fast enough to break glass. That's just smart pitching. Disguising arm velocity is not at all necessary because it will provide no clue to pitch location. So there are a few ways to simplify delivery and concentrate on the important points. You might therefore find an advantage to having a knuckleball pitcher on your staff.

· 8 ·

How to Umpire It

"You remember umpiring your first knuckleball like you remember being with your first girlfriend: you never forget it, and it's always embarrassing. I saw this ball come in, lazily swinging from side to side, and then drop like a brick. I called it the only way I could: 'Ball! Strike!' The batter looked at me and said, 'Which is it, ump?' I put my arm around his shoulder and said, 'Tell ya what, son. Would you mind taking one of each?'"—Unknown.

When you're the home-plate umpire there are only two things you need to do when you see a knuckleball coming: wait on it, and have the strike zone firmly established in your mind. We all know umpires try to make their jobs easier by trying to decide before the pitch arrives if it's a ball or strike, and some pitches far enough in or out when they are only partway home make that easy. A knuckle-ball? No way. You will *not* have any idea what it may be until it actually arrives, so wait on it until it's at the plate. The nice thing about the knuckleball, though, is that you probably won't get an argument over what it was! Most catchers don't even think about framing the strike zone, and most batters will go with whatever you call. You should have the strike zone established in your mind, but not for calling knuckleballs so much as for calling regular, garden-variety pitches. That way you may not get crossed up by the occasional fastball or curve thrown by the knuckleball pitcher—though you may have a headache when another pitcher comes in, or vice versa. You can almost hear it in the air when a knuckleball pitcher comes in or goes out in mid-game: watch how that strike zone changes! It's your job not to let it.

Outside of that, no matter where you work on the field, be ready to move. If you're behind the plate, be ready for more wild pitches and passed balls than normal. If there are men on base, this may complicate matters, so you'll have to keep a sharp eye for anything else that may affect play. If you're out in the field, you'll have to be ready to take off and call all kinds of off-field dinks, infield dribblers, and wicked shots pulled down the line. You may also get deep fly balls that may be out, off the wall, misplayed, or simply caught with ease. The toughest calls for umpires not behind the plate may be shots down the line. Despite the usual tall foul pole, you may get hard drives *over* it. When batters pull them, they're usually real screamers. Opposite-line shots are quite uncommon. You will also expect to see hits go fair but tail foul past the bag, hit something, and bounce crazily back into fair territory. Weird, unexpected bounces like this may be just as tough to call as the butterflies you'd see from behind the plate.

Umpires, like fielders, are alert for situations that may call for an inside or outside pitch, how the catcher sets up in or out, or a pitch that the pitcher wants hit in a particular direction. Don't attempt to outthink a knuckleball. Not only will it go where it wants to in or around the strike zone, but it is often not pulled or hit to the opposite field with any kind of expected pattern. To see one head for the plate as slow as it does, you may be tempted to prejudge where it may go if the batter swings. Don't try.

Knuckleballs may swing left or right a foot or more, but almost always they'll sink a foot or two. Be ready to call them around the bottom of the zone, which is tough, considering that the catcher will obscure your best view.

Try to picture your normal mental state when you're making calls behind the plate. What would you have done when Floyd Robinson swung at one that went behind him?

Do you call them if they cross any part of the plate, or just the front edge? Some umps have to be very aware of where the front edge of the plate is in order to do their job well. You may see big, hard-biting 12-6 curves once in a while, or, more commonly, low splitters that may nip the corners or edge with a sharp approach angle; but just one good knuckleball will alert you to the possibility that you'll have to keep constant focus on where those butterflies may be fluttering around the strike zone. Fortunately, everyone else may be more confused by them, so whatever you decide is usually okay.

How did Augie Donatelli handle it? Here's what he said: "The pitcher doesn't know where it's going, the hitter can't hit it, the catcher can't catch it, and it's all over the ballpark before it gets here. It's been enough places that I figure sometime on the trip it must have crossed home plate for a strike."

· 9 ·

How to Watch It

"The knuckleball needs to get more love. Until you see someone who really can throw the thing, and see it up close, you don't have the proper appreciation for it."
—Gene Lavanchy, Boston broadcaster.

If you never had a knuckleball come at you or see one wobble by you over the plate, you're missing the full flavor of the pitch. Most spectators are at a distance and to the side of the ball's path. Because of that, it's impossible for them to see the subtle little wiggle, the shift from side to side, the jump in another direction that you could see if you were on either end of one. So if you don't have a good angle on it, you're going to wonder why nobody can hit that slow pitch that seems to just lollipop on in.

It has to do with the physics of perspective and a little psychology as well.

Throw a baseball 60 feet and note how small it appears when it's caught. It should look less than one-quarter its size. Now picture a ball moving three inches to one side when it's near you, then when it's 60 feet away. It looks like it's moving a lot more when it's near you. Now, think about the reverse of that. The ball appears small at first, but then it appears to grow several times larger when it gets near you. This new perspective also magnifies any movement by several times.

Watching from the side, the ball doesn't seem to change much, and you'll have a hard time seeing any side-to-side movement of a few inches or more when you're many feet away.

It's often been reported by knuckleball pitchers playing catch that their catcher said, "Did you see that?" many more times than they said it. That's because of the perspective I've just explained. Inexperienced pitchers want to see their offering dance, but because of their perspective, it's easier for their catcher to see it. Also, taking your eyes off your target makes the ball go even crazier than it would have, so you had best let the catcher tell you how it's working. I once gave a lesson to a guy who threw what was probably the wildest knuckleball ever to come my way. We were maybe only 40 feet apart, so we wouldn't have to chase each other's butterflies much. He threw a lot of nothing pitches, then he launched one that headed toward my left shoulder. I caught it near my right knee. He never saw it take that bizarre dive.

The three people who have to deal with this pitch get the best view: catcher, umpire, and batter. The catcher is pretty close to lined up with it—as best as can be expected. The umpire, who is partially blocked by the catcher, is slightly off to one side. The batter, however, may have the toughest view of all. The difficulty is in tracking the ball well enough to judge its approach. Many batters will go for the "top-shelf cheddar," fastballs up around the letters or higher, simply because they can see them so well. Many knuckleballs will start out appearing to be up there, but then seem to take a long time showing up, and they're moving every which way at the same time. Batters also learn to judge the spin to figure out quickly what the pitch is and therefore where it may end up; try that when you not only can almost read the label but you can also see individual stitches.

The psychological part of the knuckleball's movement is the fact that, on a primitive level, you want to deal with a perceived threat. Three participants in the game have to make mental adjustments to this confusing object that's fluttering at them through the air, swooping in unpredictable ways. There's a lot of work to be done around home plate when a knuckleball comes toward it.

Ralph Kiner, as an announcer describing Phil Niekro's knuckleball: "It's a little like watching Mario Andretti park a car."

For spectators, the best view may be directly behind home plate, with some adjustment. They may be partially blocked by the umpire and the catcher, but they may get a pretty good view simply because they may be close to the plate, and the ball is coming toward them. The next-best view (or maybe the best) is a center field camera view, straightaway and slightly off to the side of the pitcher. (Those are also easier and more affordable seats to get in most major league parks.)

A few years ago I got a center-field seat, front row, at Fenway Park, when Tim Wakefield and Steve Sparks started against each other. I brought my binoculars and feasted on what may have been the best view of this butterfly showdown. The catchers' mitts looked huge, even without zooming in, and I could see how the pitches moved and where they went in the strike zone. I could see even small movements and got the best taste of the pitch of anyone in the stands.

Capturing this movement on tape is tough. For obvious reasons, the best angle is in front of the pitch as it comes straight toward the camera. Most camera people don't enjoy the thought of a four-dollar baseball intentionally thrown at a ten-thousand-dollar camera. And there's perspective again: the view of the camera may not be real life in size, so the ball not only will be smaller but its movement will appear as small.

Your best view ever of a knuckleball, therefore, is on the catching end. If you dare. When you get to see one or more live and up close, you can decide if that's the kind of pitch you'd like to be involved with. And you'll definitely have more appreciation of the art form.

The knuckleball is an obvious temptation to hitters, coming in like it's begging to be crushed. So many batters swing at it to launch it. They're often early on it, so if you're sitting near the foul line on the hitter's side, beware of foul balls pulled down that line. They *will* be dangerous. What's also dangerous is a batter who screws himself into the ground, overswinging at one he thinks he can hammer. You may hurt yourself laughing.

Can you tell when a knuckleball pitcher has thrown off all the usual negative stereotypes that people often attach to them? That's easy: when he's trusted. He'll have good outings fairly often, so anticipate some crazy hitting and foolish swings—entertaining if you're cheering on the pitcher. You may see many more out-of-control swings than usual. How batters attempt to hit the pitch will show you many examples of how not to cover the plate with a variety of adjustments in the swing. If you're trying to learn how to bat for solid contact, you may want to skip watching a knuckleballer.

If you're an outfielder, you may get to see a batted fly ball with knuckleball action, usually around the peak of its travel or slightly after it. This happens when the ball comes off the bat with little or no spin, and the airspeed of the ball slows enough to allow wind currents around it to make it jump or float. Fortunately the fly ball is high enough that this movement usually doesn't upset the fielder's chances of catching it. Outfielders throwing long toss often like to throw knucklers to each other for entertainment. You can't appreciate this unless you're under one that doesn't behave.

Experienced observers can watch pitches from behind the pitcher or catcher and have a pretty good idea how fast they are, especially at knuckleball velocities. Your most difficult viewing angle will be straight off to one side. You can tell it's a slower-than-ordinary pitch mainly because of the arc in it, but a pitcher throwing much harder than that will be difficult to judge from that angle. You'll also have no chance of seeing any of the side-to-side shift, but you can tell by the catcher's reaction where the pitch ends up.

Finding a good angle and seeing that ball dance may make you laugh or astonish you, so you may be tempted to film some pitches for home entertainment or for educational purposes. Your education will come when you view the tape. Video as well as optical technology do not combine well enough yet to truly capture any but the most insanely skittish knuckleballs, and you won't get the full flavor of live viewing. The latest developments in digital recording and HDTV offer some hope that we may be able to capture butterflies for indoor at-home enjoyment. Large-format viewing of shots from a normal lens on a camera mounted behind home plate would be the most likely way to hunt them down.

The best view a regular spectator will get is as a catcher for someone who can gently toss a few knuckleballs to them. Thrown so slowly they may not do much, if anything; but it can be amazing and hypnotic when one comes right at you, and you can clearly see the stitches and often the label too.

A freshman college pitcher once told me about an experience at his first practice. He was warming up with a few floaters, and his teammates spotted them. A few of them lined up behind the catcher and peeked around him to watch, like the Three Stooges. They were amazed, never having seen anything like a well-pitched knuckleball before, coming right at them, so they asked, "You can throw that thing for strikes?" He replied, "Sure can. And you're going to see some pretty hilarious at-bats this season." No bravado there, just the plain truth, voiced from experience.

University of Miami pitcher Sean Flaherty first saw it as a tyke, on television, in a bar, where his father took him (out of elementary school, by the way) to watch Charlie Hough start the Marlins' first-ever game. Sean was impressed, at an age you wouldn't expect most kids to appreciate such a thing.

If you can round up someone who can throw a knuckleball, and you can throw them yourself, a short-distance game of catch will amuse you more than most spectators, and it may be the seed of greater things. Phil Niekro and his father used to throw them to each other, and Phil and brother Joe naturally played catch with it. So did Tim Wakefield and his father. Most of those I've met who throw them are purely recreational pitchers, toying with them for entertainment and not from a mound in an organized game. Nothing wrong with that. Because of the nature of the beast, even just goofing with them can leave a lasting impression. I told you about the wildest one I ever saw, and it was from a raw amateur. So if you think you won't ever see a world-class knuckleball because you haven't seen a major league pitcher throw one, you just haven't seen enough knuckleballs yet.

Watching batters swing may clue you in on how the pitcher is doing. If you see a lot of swings down on the ball or misses by a lot, you may see a no-hitter in the making. Level swings are the second-best kind for the pitcher; they might produce a lower than average number of runs, considering the fact that so many knuckleballs are sinking more than most pitches. If you want a home run souvenir, sit outside the fences when you see a lot of upper-cut golf swings. Then you'll see many fly balls and maybe too many souvenirs for this pitcher to last long.

Since it takes mid-teenage velocity, and deception that can be learned at any age, is it possible to see a high-schooler—male or female—who is ready for the majors? Likely, no. Players destined for the majors are rare. Possible? Of course! If they learn to deceive well at an early age, their knuckleball develops as they grow, and they get the support of coaches who understand what they see and not hold a prejudice, you may see a ballplayer who is on the fast track to the major leagues. It's said that catcher is the position easiest to take to the majors, but the major leagues can never have enough good pitching. Because the physical stress on a knuckleball pitcher is less than on other pitchers, they're not as likely to wind up on the disabled list due to injury or fatigue, and slow down their development. While no one takes up the knuckleball first and foremost out of fear of injury, it's a welcome side effect. *(Two terms never associated with a knuckleball pitcher: Tommy John and rotator cuff surgery. Those two end many budding careers. One term always associated with a knuckleballer: can pitch a lot of innings.)* If you see a teen who is smart on the mound, can throw for outs, and has just average speed, all that's left is an interest on the part of a major league scout, and astonishing things can happen right before your eyes.

· 10 ·

The History

No one knows for sure who threw the first knuckleball. A case can be made for nineteenth-century pitcher Toad Ramsey, who as a youth severed a tendon in the middle finger of his pitching hand. He pitched by resting that finger on the ball and gripping it with the inside of his index and ring fingers. This sure looks and sounds like a form of forkball, but it is possible to throw a no-spin pitch that way. He had a pretty impressive record over a long career, so he must have been able to control the pitch with reliability. (The grips shown here are approximate models of those used by the players described. Notice there is no *one* knuckleball grip. Each pitcher found a grip that worked for *him and his individual mechanics*.)

Ed Summers may have been the first to throw it with curled fingers, but it was probably Eddie Cicotte of the White Sox who was the first to champion it. He may have tried a few different grips in his career, as evidenced by several surviving pictures, with a solid pitching record to prove his ability to master it.

Eddie Cicotte

During this time period—the early 1900s—the spitball was still legal, and the game was played with general contempt for home run hitters. (It was thought that anyone could hit a homer, but it took real skill to play the game within the general area of the infield.) As a result, whatever the pitchers could do to fool batters was considered fair game, so this may have been the golden age of the knuckleball. Surely many pitchers were throwing it at the time, but few were interested in revealing the secret weapon they may have been using. An interesting note: the pitch was then variously known as a knuckleball, a dry spitter, a floater, or a dancer.

Into the 1920s and 1930s you might have seen future Hall of Famers Ted Lyons and Jessie Haines throwing it, but there were others, colorful characters all: "Fat Freddie" Fitzsimmons, Schoolboy Rowe, Eddie Rommel, Nap Rucker, and "Willie the Knuck" Ramsdell, to mention just a few.

Wartime in the early 1940s brought on some interesting situations involving knuckleball pitchers. The Negro Leagues, who put on a talent exhibition as much as a baseball game, showcased future Hall of Famer Cool Papa Bell as well as Ray Brown and Jim "Fireball" Cohen. (We can only imagine the ugly swings induced by someone nick-named "Fireball" if he mixed in a knuckleball.) The Washington Senators could boast *four* starting knuckle-ballers: Johnny Niggeling, Roger Wolfe, Emil "Dutch" Leonard, and Mickey Haefner.

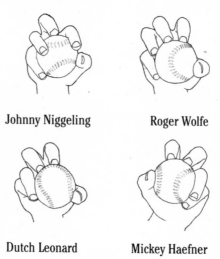

Johnny Niggeling   Roger Wolfe

Dutch Leonard   Mickey Haefner

Future Hall of Famer Early Wynn was also on the Senators at this time. It's reported that Wynn didn't throw a knuckleball as his primary pitch, as the others did, but he did throw some.

Early Wynn

The most successful pitcher of this era may have been a member of the All-American Girls Professional Baseball League, Annabelle "Lefty" Lee, who threw the first perfect game in league history. Apparently her talent for entertainment and upsetting opposing batters rubbed off on her nephew, future major leaguer Bill Lee.

Postwar, the two best knuckleballers may have been Leonard and Gene Bearden of the Cleveland Indians, who had one immense season, ending in a playoff win against the Red Sox. In 1952, Bobby Shantz was MVP with his simple but effective game plan of getting ahead in the count, then throwing a knuckler to finish the batter off.

Gene Bearden

A number of pitchers threw at least some knuckleballs at this time, attempting to either continue careers or get an edge on the better hitters of the time. Hoyt Wilhelm was the first to capture the imagination of youngsters when, on nationwide television, he no-hit the Yankees when pitching for the Orioles. He was probably the first to be called a "pure" knuckleball pitcher. He threw them at least 80 percent of the time and used the knuckler as his bread-and-butter pitch in virtually every tight situation. Wilhelm is generally regarded as the modern caretaker of the knuckleball. Many knuckleball pitchers since his retirement have worn his uniform number 49 to honor him.

Hoyt Wilhelm

You'd probably figure that the winningest brother act in major league history would have to use a baffling pitch like the knuckleball, and you'd be correct. Hall of Famer Phil Niekro and brother Joe won 539 games between them from the early 1960s to the late 1980s. In this age of television, their performances both separately and against each other made for great theater. They are two of the most storied of all knuckleballers.

Phil Niekro　　　　　Joe Niekro　　　　　Wilbur Wood

For showing just how tough you could pitch with a knuckleball, there may have been none better than Wilbur Wood. Often pitching on two days' rest, Wood won 20 or more games four years straight for the White Sox, and once started both ends of a doubleheader. He was also one of the few lefties to throw it, and undoubtedly the most successful.

Recent pitchers who have thrown at least one include—believe it or not—John Smoltz, Bob Gibson, Jose Canseco, Mickey Lolich, and Todd Zeile. And . . . Wade Boggs?

Wade Boggs

Jim Bouton

Then there's Jim Bouton. He made his name not so much for his record with the Yankees, Pilots, and Braves. He wrote what's considered one of the top 100 books of the twentieth century, *Ball Four*. He continues to have success off the field, further contributing to the game as a writer and businessman.

When you think of the Oakland A's of the 1990s you likely think of heavy hitters, but Tom Candiotti was throwing a knuckler for them as well as anyone in the American League, with the possible exception of Charlie Hough.

Tom Candiotti

Charlie Hough

It's said that the knuckleball pitcher is a dying breed. Perhaps not. While Steve Sparks has had some success for a decade, the current best practitioner of the art is, no question, Red Sox ace Tim Wakefield. A protégé of Hoyt Wilhelm but more directly Phil Niekro, Tim was nearly MVP of the 1991 playoffs while pitching for the Pirates. Since going to Boston, he has gone through a learning curve like many of his breed, but he has come through to have a feel and understanding of the pitch like few in major league history, with success to match.

Steve Sparks   Tim Wakefield

How he pitches will surely rub off on others if it hasn't already influenced the likes of Jared Fernandez and a few up-and-coming talented pitchers in the minors, such as Red Sox farmhand Charlie Zink.

Jared Fernandez   Charlie Zink

Thanks to modern communications, the future is bright for anyone who wants to learn the pitch or hobnob with fellow knights of the knuckleball. The internet has a wealth of stats on each of the more than 100 pitchers who threw at least one in the major leagues and fan sites devoted to some. A web search will find the very complete and chatty KnuckleballHQ. The Hall of Fame has inducted seven pitchers who threw it, and its website provides accompanying biographies and data. And now you can say someone wrote the book on it.

· 11 ·

How to Chart a Knuckleball Pitcher

Key stats will indicate how a knuckleball pitcher is performing. While it's been said that an elite knuckleballer can put up power-pitcher numbers, that's rare and not completely accurate when it comes to judging long-term effectiveness.

The numbers are likely to reflect something more in line with Greg Maddux over the long term: few walks, a half-dozen or more strikeouts per game, lots of swinging strikes and badly hit balls. Pitch count is an exception: because of the easy motion and low arm stress, a knuckleballer can go deeper into a game without struggling due to fatigue.

After years of studying the elite of the game, I think these key stats tell whether a guy's got it or not:

Walks per nine innings: no more than two. If batters are patient and having long at-bats, this is a fabulous number to look at. If pitch counts are limited per game, or complete games go seven innings in your league, another way to look at this is walks per hundred pitches, which should be roughly not much more than two. Three or more may indicate trouble.

Wild pitches: no more than one per nine innings.

Strikeouts: six per nine innings. Naturally, more is better, but sometimes this is a matter of luck. Six is reasonable for any pitcher in control of the game from first out to last.

WHIP (walks plus hits per innings pitched): keep it to one or less. The lower, the better. 1.3 or higher is a problem.

Wins/losses: depends to a great extent on his team's defensive effectiveness combined with offensive production, so it's not a good pitcher stat.

ERA: WHIP is a better indicator, but an ERA of better than league average is what counts.

First-pitch strikes: I don't care what you pitch, this should be at least 90 percent. First-pitch strikes are almost always a free gift and an easy way to set up the rest of the at-bat. One major league team is said to require all its minor league batters always to take the first pitch. Any team going to bat with this program is telling you they're giving you at least 27 free gifts per game! Make them knuckleballs!

Strikes/balls ratio: at least 2 to 1. The higher the percentage, the better, provided it's accompanied by a good WHIP.

Pitches per nine innings: 110 is average, many lower means the batters are not patient at the plate, and that's more a function of batter impatience and lack of pitch judgment than a pitcher's handiwork. For leagues that may limit a pitcher's count in a game, you can translate this to roughly 12 pitches per inning. More per inning or nine innings isn't the problem here as it is with other pitchers who are taking more out of their arms on each outing. You can use this stat to compare the effectiveness of the knuckleball pitcher relative to others, or the patience (or lack thereof) of the batters he faces. You may find that batters seeing a swarm of knuckleballs for the first time are impatient, and the count may be low. But expect batters' first adjustment to be patience. They'll go deeper into the count, looking for better pitches or genuine strikes. A knuckleball pitcher in shape, in control, and focused from start to finish should be able to throw more than 125 pitches in a game without physical harm. Just watch out for the first signs of fatigue when the pitch count gets high—but that's true for any pitcher.

Which stats are most revealing? Low walks per nine innings, wild pitches below one per game, and WHIP.

As we've said before, an elite knuckleball pitcher will give up an odd mix of strangely hit balls: infield dinks, pop-ups, easy fly balls, screamers pulled down the line— and about as many home runs as a top-level power pitcher. A lot of lame ground balls indicates the batters are topping the ball, which is good until they adjust, so enjoy the moment but be alert to make an adjustment.

· 12 ·

You Know the Drill?

A few simple yet highly effective drills can help anyone master the knuckleball. These are meant to help you understand it more than to develop muscles, so you may prefer to call them fun flutterball activities.

The first drill can be done anywhere you have a few feet of headroom above you. Take a baseball with any knuckleball grip of your choosing, and try to toss it in the air a few feet without letting it rotate. You'll quickly find two elements that make almost all the difference: the ball must be released from tight against the palm, and if you flip it without bending your wrist at all, it should come pretty straight off your fingertips and fly high with little or no rotation. If you have a high ceiling, it may be fun to see how high you can toss it without rotation. This will teach you two important elements of throwing it in a normal horizontal direction and still keeping the spin off. This is useful just to learn the basics by yourself; constantly doing this drill may mess up your normal throwing.

If you have a catcher, you can try a short-distance

game of catch, or, if you're ready for the next level, a game of Hot Potato, which is just trying to get off as many knuckleball tosses as fast as you can. Don't throw hard, just get them away quickly. Doing this over a short distance will allow you to watch the ball a little and help you develop a rhythm so that you'll grip the ball the same way every time. The orientation of the seams is unimportant here. You may elect to use this drill as a warm-up, then gradually back away to full pitching distance if you can keep the rotation off the ball. It's an excellent confidence builder and allows you to notice the feel of the release that works for you, so you'll have no need to watch the ball to know you got off a good one.

You can take this one level higher by getting together with another knuckleballer to see if you can throw pitches that especially fool the other guy or have particular movement. Having someone on the other end who knows something about the knuckleball who wants to work on it himself may result in your quickest and most effective lessons. You'll have an opportunity to swap ideas and ask each other, "How did you throw that one?"

It may help either of these drills—and it could be fun—if you make "my ball Spot." Using a felt-tip marker—black preferred—mark spots on the ball a quarter-turn apart, all around. There will be six spots total. Make them about the size of a dime. You can use this ball to better judge rotation. Optionally, you can color the seams black.

You may find that your best training aids are either fresh brand-new balls with small seams, or old, soaked-and-dried ones you find in the woods near a local park. A minor league pitcher told me he loved the low seams on major league balls that he tried; his fingernails didn't catch on the seams as much, so he had more confidence and more effectiveness. Just starting off, you may like the high seams of an old weather-beaten ball, because it may produce some jaw-dropping sashays that will really give you confidence and help you develop your pitch so you can throw it for strikes.

I wouldn't necessarily recommend fingertip pushups, but there's a lot to be said for developing strong fingers. Working them in some way to develop a sure and delicate and controlled feel should help. Some knuckleball pitchers play guitar or a musical instrument that demands extensive finger movement; if you don't find them boring, simple finger-strengthening exercises can help. No one has come up with a way to help preserve and strengthen fingernails with much effectiveness, but I own a game-used bat that Phil Niekro taped a pad to, a sure way to protect those vital two fingertips of his. If you don't worry about harming your knuckleball when batting, you're more likely to take batting practice and maybe learn batting well enough to figure out how to counteract it with smart pitching. Not enough pitchers study the enemy with a war club in hand.

One last drill that demands an explanation: A mysterious overcast of close, low cloud cover was flowing by overhead, not more than a hundred feet above a coastal Maine farmhouse one late summer afternoon. I was about ten, and my father and I were on the front lawn, looking up at the strange clouds. My father said, "Those are the kinds of

clouds that make tornadoes." So it was with a little con-
cern that I began catching pitches that my father threw to
me. No one had ever shown me what different pitches did,
and I wasn't the greatest at catching them. I had no idea
what was in store, and this was starting to be too much for
my youthful inexperience—until he threw me one pitch
that was as strange and mysterious as the sky above. I
could see seams, and the ball gave a few wiggles on the
way in. Baseballs can't do that! He explained that this
weird pitch was called a knuckleball, and that it was especially tough to hit, but when hit solid, it really flies. I was
fascinated.

It took far too many years for me to learn all about this
goofy knuckleball thing, but I finally have, I think.

So what's the drill? Simply this: go throw one to a
child. If it does what baseballs can't do and ignites a lifetime of curiosity and fascination (and maybe a career
throwing them or writing about them), then that one pitch
has blossomed into something very special for that child
and the person who threw it.

For this drill, that one pitch, that's everything.

Index

A NOTE ON THE AUTHOR

Dave Clark was born in Fitchburg, Massachusetts, grew up there, and went to school in the area. He has been a woodworker, ceramic furnace operator, car salesman, skydiving instructor, radio announcer, comedy writing instructor, parachute designer and assembler, chemical batch maker, forklift operator, hockey referee, Zamboni driver, produce deliverer, and amateur open-mike comedian. He is currently a professional photographer and lives in Barre, Massachusetts, with his wife, son, and daughter. He spends most of his time thinking about knuckle-balls.